BECOMING A BUTTERFLY
FROM PRISON TO PH.D.

DR. NKRUMAH LEWIS

ISBN-10: 0615575994
ISBN-13: 978-0615575995

DEDICATION

This work is dedicated to every little boy, trapped inside the body of a man without vision, who does not see the strength in tears, the joy in anguish, the validation in lies, the victory in sound and certain defeat, and the beauty of suffering. To you I say, resist grounding; arise and fly.

CONTENTS

ACKNOWLEDGMENTS

First and foremost, I am thankful to the Most High for having entrusted me with the trials that are chronicled in the pages that are to follow. I am convinced that He invested in me abilities that were called forth and enhanced by what many would label as suffering. A very special thanks goes out to "daddy's girls", D'Malyah, D'Ara, and Madison, for showing me what unconditional love was, humanizing me with compassion and allowing me to share your childhood and see things for the very first time through your eyes. Everything that I do is for you. I would like to thank Dr. Tracie Olds Lewis, Tosha Jones and Ursula Littlejohn for indulging my requests to read early versions of this work with candor. I would like to thank Eric Crawford, Henry "Hank" Wall and Dr. Manuel Dudley for mentorship in the discipline of life matters. I would like to thank Broderick Self, Mike Redmon and Eddie Ellis, Jr. for never forsaking the brotherhood and daring me to dream beyond the confines of our past. I love you all.

I would like to thank Daryl Shaw for partnering his genius with the vision God placed in my heart. Thank you for your meticulous care and ear as we ran this last mile. Thank you to Pastors Montey Lewis, Michael Cotton and Jayson Sloan for praying a hedge of protection all around me as I found my way and answered the call on my life. Thank you for challenging me, cultivating my theology and reminding me of whose I was.

All great journeys have their incipience. Therefore, I would like to thank "Godfather" and "Stan" for being my guardian angels and investing time in me as you did your time. I lie awake some nights wondering what God showed you to have you nurture me in the animalistic environment that was our residence of steel, or if either of you were ever really real. I wish to thank Drs. Carol Bailey, Terry Kershaw, Rebecca Adams, and Kenneth Allan for grooming me, not only in formal process of education, but in the transformative matters of race relations. I would like to thank every single person that continually inquired about this project and admonished me to see it to fruition. Lastly, thanks to every student that has ever sat in one of my classes and endured me and returned to spend time in fellowship not because it was a requirement, but because you recognized our meeting was not pure happenstance. I salute you and thank you for allowing me to impart my life's lessons into your spirits.

INTRODUCTION

As we situate our lives against the backdrop of time, we are left with the conclusion that the brevity of our days on earth are but a whisper. Along this abbreviated pathway, we are often overtaken with the difficulties of the trek, and seldom if ever slow our pace to consume the scenery that is life. Our experiences color our innocence and make pale our humanity. Just as we pause to take stock of our purpose; seemingly, the curtain closes. Many of us, hold fast to the belief that our identity is one of victim, and life has happened to us, but those who are stars, whom enter our world and use their gravitational pull of affinity for change, awakening us to the living of life, no matter how momentary, are the ones we honor long after they are gone.

This notion of purpose has visited with me since I was a child. It is often that I tell those searching for direction that their passion is found amidst their pain. I have navigated a myriad of harsh realisms, teetering betwixt a plane of spiritual beliefs and bitter realities. I have experienced homelessness, child abuse, incarceration, multiple suicide attempts and the street gang lifestyle. If this is as far as you read, then of course my life would sound just like several million others that call America home. As Dr. David Jeremiah states in one of his aptly entitled books, I was "captured by grace". I have come to the conclusion that the aforementioned emotional traumas have caused limbic schisms in my memory that bang against the walls of my mind as open doors in the dead of winter; yet I long to leave a footprint of truths on this land that might never be removed.

Upon first glance, the reader would surely comment that my life has been a series of disappointments, betrayals and attempts to extinguish my own life because of self-loathing. At different junctures, I too have shared the exact same prospect. It is however, the journey back to and beyond my former self that has reckoned me to believe that my life has instead been a carefully orchestrated plan with undeniable evidences of divine intervention at almost every turn. Quite simply put, nothing occurs by happenstance. When moments in my life are at a loss for activity, I reflect upon the years that require my mind to stretch forth its recall. There are instances that I have repressed and placed in my cerebral closet, opting never to don them again…until now.

When asked these days about the concept of regret, and having the ability to do things over or differently, I reply in all sincerity, that "I would not". This is of course prefaced with the heavy heartedness of having caused so much destruction, pain, and being the precipitator of enumerable violent interactions. More than anything, I know for certain that this path, as sordid as it was, is inextricably fused to my destiny. A great many of my days and years, for that matter, have been wasted asking "why". "Why is this happening to me?" "What did I do to deserve this?" "Will things ever get better?" "How can God, who is supposed to be so loving, allow such things to befall me?" The answers have led me to the brink of insanity and ultimately to the fountains of solace.

The most profound epiphany that I have had has been one of an abstract nature. For all of the catch phrases, poetry, literary citations and the like that assert that we are in control of our lives, I find that to be but partially true. Life is not a whimsical state of being, whereby things occur without rhyme or reason; that is not what I mean at all. Quite frankly, I firmly believe that we are creatures that are subject to a greater power, which I reverence as Yahweh (The Most High). Philosophers and pontificators, of greater merits than I, would perhaps seek to deconstruct my statement for the sake of debate, citing that I have in essence given myself over to the notion that life is predestined, and that man is not always a creature of free will or rational choice.

While there are choices and decisions to be made daily and instantaneously, these choices, when not properly aligned with the perfect will of God for our lives create deviations from our destiny that become more and more difficult to recover from. I have tasted tears as bitter as the stench of death and alternatively been allowed to rest my feet on clouds. While I feel most times as though I have lived a millennium, I am constantly refreshed by what life has yet to offer me.

My mind is constantly overrun with the full gamete of emotions. Many days I incessantly plummet myself into work. On other days, I am content to sit idly, enamored with the simplicity of the sun shining; a blessing of which I was deprived during most of my incarceration, because my maximum security cell faced a wall. I am completely enraptured with nature and the sophistication of our world. All around me, people are moving and posturing within the strata, on their way to some non-descript destination, yet spending most of their lives bewildered as to how to get there. Since I was a toddler, I have never had a problem dreaming. In classes, I would drift far away, beyond the reach of the teacher's voice, and visualize myself standing before thousands of people delivering a rousing oratory that would admonish people to zealously pursue their promise.

The two earliest and most profound influences on my life were the infamous leaders Malcolm X, and Dr. Martin Luther King, Jr. As opposed to playing outdoors, I read books that chronicled the Civil Rights Movement. I was awe stricken by how the two commanded the English language in such a manner as to make people move their feet and walk headlong into unfavorable consequences. I longed to embody Malcolm's strength, fervor and commitment to resist with every fiber of his being, along with Dr. King's charismatic amicability and both vibrant and superior speaking couplet. While some might think it odd, it was an innate compulsion to in some way galvanize my generation since I was a child.

Somewhere along the line, those influences would become individuals that were a presence of marked resistance and who articulated the suffering that had entered my life; men like Mike Tyson, and rappers such as Tupac Shakur and DMX. The manner in which they spoke of their pain became the proverbial soundtrack for my life. I would live out the authenticity of their lyrics and/or public tirades. I felt like a rebel without pause, and my life, at least for a time became meaningless. Hence, the rationale that underlies my crafting of this book is to help both readers, and I understand how it is that I was able to return again to my path of true purpose.

As I engage in radio and news interviews, the question never fails to be asked, as to how I ultimately turned things around.

In the heat of the moment, I inevitably posit some crafted and concise response, so as not to waste air time. Alternatively, in retrospect, I languish for the rest of that day, in and out of daydreams, recalling the activities in which I had once been such a willing participant, and hope that I might find some structured pattern for success. In all altruism, these last two decades of my life have been a blur, and innately people, such as I, want nothing more than to distance ourselves from a past identity of which we are not proud.

I will always recall, sitting in a classroom on the campus of my alma mater, UNC Greensboro, listening to Kirk Bloodsworth, the first man freed from death row because of DNA evidence, place into context the marriage of my past and purpose. Kirk had wrongly been convicted on several occasions of the brutal rape and murder of a little girl in Maryland. He proffered that he had spent so many years running from his past, and living somewhat as a recluse, that his greatest victories have come, running towards it.

As it is with Kirk, I have deduced that the time has come for me to embrace my yesterdays, and with all the vigor that I can muster, run towards them. So many people in a myriad of situations need desperately to know that they are not alone in their struggles, and that someone has indeed acted on their innermost thoughts, and survived to tell a tale of success. In the coming pages, I will share the darkest memories of my life and then, the principles and concepts that have led to my personal renaissance and empowerment. It is my hope that this work would touch the weary traveler and revive their dreams, and that they too would writhe free of the burdensome shackles of this life that encumber their destinies and take flight.

In a world of individualism and social ill that threatens to usurp the remnant of goodwill and humanity left in this Earth, I have become a gross dichotomy of the two polar forces. The pages that are forthcoming, tell tales of utter anguish and pain that has nearly vanquished my breath; a heart that beats on the strength of hope and a will born of an internal desire to manifest outward redemption. The purpose for this literary offering of my life's story is solely to encourage the fatigued and battle scarred to realize their greatest greatness. Life shall not have the last laugh, for our latter days can most assuredly be greater than our former.

In some senses, I have scribed this work as a therapeutic modality to self-medicate my tortured soul. In addition, this is an attempt to exorcise my mind of travails, that until now, I denied the effect of. Scar tissue remains from life's worst blows and my deeds number among the things we call iniquity. I have heaped the loathing of others and my own self-hatred upon my shoulders and dared to march forward in search of my calling. Slowly and without flinching, I have kissed the lips of grace and known fleeting serenity.

Contained herein, perhaps you and I might find our faces, attempt to find the courage to withstand times of turbulence, wrought with insurmountable odds and emerge victorious on the sands of success. We must then return to confront our darkest hours and bring others into the marvelous light. There are those who have warned me of the potential costs of penning such book. There have been those in higher positions than I, that have attempted to mute the pages that are to come in fear of what the perception might be, or how my affiliation with them might be blighted. In faith, I have opted for the route of transparency, for in our midst a great many ache in misguided silence under the premise that their anguish is unique to them and them alone. I simply say, "I have no choice" and "God will protect me".

This is likely the most difficult endeavor of my existence and the toll that has been taken on my life is incalculable. I have admittedly wanted to quit and cast this work to the side and suffer in silence. I can truly emote that I have never known the resistance of principalities and imaginations to this magnitude. I believe that this book is a semblance of penance, and my trepidation and fears regarding it are of no consequence. At times, we must simply carry out orders while our heart is torn asunder.

As a witness of hope, through my pain and weakness, I shall bear the backlashes of this lifetime in so that you might be made strong. I have determined in my being that in order that my suffering is not in vain, it must be of some benefit, even if in some miniscule manner. I am incessantly in search of my place in the universe, longing to strike a harmonious balance with both nature and man. I know now because of incarceration that I must reverence time, appreciating all that is consumed through my eye gates. As for man, due to the violence and hurt that has reverberated throughout and from my person, I can no longer in good faith be a voyeur of pain and fail to be a part of the solution. Towards this end, I dedicate my entire existence and lay down my life.

EGG STAGE

During the first life stage of butterflies, an egg is laid without protection of the undercarriage of a plant, which also serves as a food source. It is also proffered that the butterfly that lays the egg has to make a decision as to whether to lay more eggs or fly off again. The egg is thus left unprotected, shielded from the world and its elements, only by a tiny shell.

CHAPTER 1: BECOMING A BUTTERFLY

As if it were but yesterday, I can remember being the tender age of nine and riding my bicycle in the country at my grandparents' house, far away from reality, far away from the trouble that lay in my future. Life was uncompromisingly simplistic then; there were no worries regarding the provision of my care. Amidst the hues of summer days, the heat poured over my shoulders; I felt both free and embraced. My elder cousin and I would find a spot in the grass, and lie on our backs studying the clouds and staring into the sun until we could no longer see. My, how I wished I could be situated amongst the heavens. I suppose like every child, I wanted to be the fictional character, Superman, so that I might know what it was to glide amidst the great beyond. Experience and injury would serve as a harsh teacher that tying towels around my neck and leaping from great heights could not accomplish my goal of flight.

My mind trailed the sky like the planes that wrote in them. Closer still were flying things, birds, mosquitoes and butterflies. Everything seemed to be going about some manner of business, either in search of food, or fleeing some predator. The butterfly was the only specimen that was childlike, frolicking to and fro, consuming the beauty of its surroundings, unaware and innocent. Even more, the butterfly was a manifestation of freedom, possessing all colors, belonging to none. Oh how I longed to become a butterfly. I think of it now and fancy myself idealistic and perhaps even foolish to entertain the notion of flying, and for that fact true freedom.

I felt bound to earth by my African American ancestry and grounded by the social construction of the misnomer of race. It occurred to me as well, that throughout our history, freedom had been bartered for blood, and butterflies don't bleed. I will never forget watching a childhood friend catch one (a butterfly) by its wings and watching as it writhed and struggled to be free from his grasp. It was alive, vibrant and longing to be let go and return to its purpose; to saddle the breeze and ride. The oil from my friend's hands had soiled its wings until they had been damaged. I felt horrible as I observed its failed attempts to resume its rightful place in nature's backdrop; it was not to be. What he did that day became eerily prophetic for my own life. I would be soiled and damaged by life's experiences and unable to fly.

As an adult I once looked my mother unflinchingly in her eyes, and prodded, "Why didn't you love me the same (as my brothers)?" Her face escaped my piercing glance, as I had purposed it to singe her heart with the guilt of my sufferings. I was cognitively startled when she gently replied, "you know, you look at all of your children, and a parent knows who the strong one is and which one needs her most. You didn't need us." As quickly as I had believed I had wittingly posed a question, to which there could be no adequate retort, the rage and resentment I had harbored for my parents for years had subsided.

During my years of gang affiliation and visits to penal institutions, my parents and I would pass each other in public places without a word, yet saying so much; silent yelling and the muted hurling of accusations as to which of us had been inept at the foreign precept of love. I would search my mother's face for a semblance of the anguish that I felt from our being torn apart by circumstances born of my father's hand. Needless to say, while I can make no claim to identify with the magnanimous suffering that biblical figures such as Job endured, I am familiar with the despair of being resolved to the original state of matter from which I was first contrived; an egg left unprotected, naked and alone.

My earliest recollection of passage was so abrupt and disconcerting that it has found permanent residence in the inner-most parts of my mind...my memory. I was an awkward and unsure child, caught between antithetical realities that tortured my existence. On the one hand, I was the first and most loved grandchild, and had been coddled, spoiled and nurtured by my grandparents down in the eastern part of the state where everything was slow, until I attained the age of five. On the other hand, I was well read, knowledgeable of how to spell my African name and scheduled to return to a wildly city upbringing in Durham, North Carolina.

Durham was a major hub of Tobacco production during my childhood. I can recall lying in daycare at Bright World on my blue cot for naptime, and everyday around one o'clock smelling the sweet aroma of tobacco being manufactured downtown. That smell carried across town from Liggett & Myers into my daycare and seduced me during naps as I dreamed of mythical places and playing outside. My favorite part of daycare was story time. My fascination with verbiage had its origin early on. My interests were quite different from those of other children though.

In my formative years, the books that I read immortalized Dr. King, Malcolm X, and the Kennedy brothers as human rights giants. The manner in which they were all killed saddened me even as a boy that could not quite grasp the deep-seated hatred that characterized the South in which I lived. I had also deduced for myself that white America hated black folk just because they were black, and those that empathized with the struggle for civil rights were as brutally hated.

I had very strong opinions and a wisdom that outdated me. I recall a teacher asking me what I wanted to be when I grew up. At five years old, I responded that I wanted to be a martyr. She was astonished and told my mother; to which my mother angrily remarked, "let someone else's child die for black people." At this point, I had surmised that if I could survive my own blackness, I would do something great for black America, even if it cost me my life.

It was my little brother six years my junior that morphed into the sea of faces at the Lincoln Memorial in 1963, and a pile of books from my small white bookcase that provided me the pseudo platform to challenge the Negro still oblivious to his social castration. I donned blankets upon my frail shoulders with broom in hand, as I emulated those strong black faces that commanded my attention situated on the Great Kings of Africa posters produced by Budweiser. It was during these moments that I felt most alive, filled with purpose and destined to propel myself beyond my familial circumstance and stride into that galactic place called greatness.

Alternatively, for the greater amount of my rearing, my self-esteem remained in shambles as a youth. Violence enveloped my life on a day to day basis and I found it hard to catch my breath. I could not escape its grasp. It was a cloud that shadowed my every movement. When I inhaled deeply and reckoned myself to a cause, I found the taste of tears in my mouth. I didn't understand violence at the time, so it was an experience of shock and dismay each time that I encountered my would-be friend. I recall being so confused and coming not only to loathe my surroundings, but myself. I was always careful not to misstep. This paranoia and tentativeness was only exacerbated as I interacted with other children.

I learned quickly that violence was the preferable method of resolving problems, and that it was also a way to garner the "respect" of others. There was a kid named "Man" that would terrorize all of the children his age and younger, taking our lunch money and other valuables such as marbles. I remember envying the freedom he had, being able to run all over the neighborhood, having no curfew, hanging with the high-school kids and even cussing freely and without consequence. I wished I was "Man." He had failed his grade at least twice by the time I came to his attention, and I was no different from the rest. I was his victim. I even resorted to getting off at another bus stop, and trying to cut through the neighbors' yards to avoid the inevitable.

I will never forget, coming home at twelve years old, out of breathe and my mother standing at the door. "Where are you coming from?" "You ran home didn't you?" "You got one more day to come home running, or crying because somebody beat your tail, and I am going to beat it again!" I went into my room and closed the door, and practiced fighting the air, and pillows. The next morning, I went to the bus stop, and challenged "Man" to a fight, and won. That evening on the bus, he was being teased about the loss that morning and tried to save face by engaging me in another confrontation. He lost again and again, because I began jumping on him at random over the years.

That day marked the birth of my dichotomous being and for years the twain would fail to meet. I learned at that very intersection in my life, several things about violence. Violence is the cessation of all verbal negotiations; violence garners respect for the winner, and marks the loser a target for further violence; violence is cyclical; violence is learned; violence gets you what you want without having to ask nicely; and the consequences of violence seldom outweigh the benefit to the user. This is how I began to conceptualize violence, and how I would utilize it to my benefit throughout the course of my life.

By the age of 17, I would have no place to call home, and would have a heart as black as a thousand midnights. I had fully been so consumed by violence that the only thing that surpassed my volatility was the precision and planning with which I carried it out. The moment that I lost complete control of my faculties and stepped into animalism was during a confrontation with a guy that had attacked me over eight years prior. He was fourteen at the time, and I was nine. He had jumped on me after school and badly injured my leg. I approached him and asked if he remembered me as we played pick-up basketball at a local gymnasium. He casually replied that he didn't remember me. I took a bat that I had, and drove nails through the end of it that evening. I returned the next day and beat him until my shirt turned from white to pink.

I had developed a rebellious spirit, a disdain for authority and refused to pause for direction from anyone, especially a father that I resented perhaps more than I loved myself. A final violent confrontation with my father marked my entrée into manhood. More wounded than all was my connection to my mother, as I took a peremptorily glance at her sobbing face realizing that she was powerless in this situation; she would have to defend herself from his abuse now. I began breaking into newly constructed houses and abandoned cars for a few hours sleep. Stealing and selling drugs were the methods that I developed to subsidize my survival. I used violence to solidify my standing in the streets, and was known for being able to handle myself, even when the odds were not in my favor.

I began carrying guns, knives, and even a machete, which further imploded my reputation as someone who "didn't give a f*ck", and was "down for whatever." The more outlandish the behavior, the more appealing, I thought. The key component to my survival at that time was aligning myself with others like me, and this is what I did. It was the aroma of the housing projects that beckoned my presence. Here I would find a group of young boys that had garnered a reputation for the despicable and irrational. We were the kids that I shake my head in disbelief at today. Our appetite for unprovoked and retaliatory violence was egregious; this rebellion could not be quelled, for it raged like the fires of hell from within us.

I had no reverence for death, and I often invited it, especially when a gun was aimed at my countenance. This was often the time during which I became the most emboldened. The pain of being nothing, of having no identity and hating who I was and could never be, consumed me. I joined the military and was later incarcerated there. This would be one of many times. Though the incarceration was later adjudicated wrongful, it nonetheless introduced me to a more philosophical and intimate conception of what true violence was, and how it was contrived and manifest. It was here that an elderly white man told me why he had murdered his wife and castrated the man she was caught being unfaithful with. He said "justice by the hands of man is the most thorough." Those words have never departed my mind.

As I think about all of the crimes that I have committed and all of the mayhem that I have been responsible for, I am left with the thought, that because I perceived that I had been wronged, and felt a myriad of discomforting emotions, who else could adequately administer justice that could quench my desire for retribution, or for that matter, heal my wounded pride? I forged my existence into a weapon and pointed it at anyone that posed a resistance or appeared weak; this was my measure of justice for being ignored and abused. My greatest defiance would be in the face of whites. They represented an unknown perpetrator of great indignities to me, and this was constantly reinforced by the rhetoric of older blacks whom I overheard talking. I attended school for the greater part of my life never having had to interact or socialize with whites. I perceived that my personal plight was such that it was because of their historic oppression and I resented them for it. They had turned brothers against brothers and fathers against sons.

This is what drove me; a fury and a passion so deep that I had once believed that I was possessed by something not of this world. It frequently failed me how another man lay beneath my feet unconscious and bleeding. Imagine for a few seconds, being inebriated with revenge, and feeling that in one instance that you were a deity capable of swift, tactical and decisive measures against the grandest of your enemies. For years, I would envision "Man" taunting me or my father's face in place of my victims', as I poured out my wrath on the mirrored image of my aching soul. For me, violence was a language. It communicated my hurt, anger, frustration, envy, and hatred.

Armed with derision for authority and an internal mechanism for justifying my own actions, violence made me feel a power that was foreign to me; that was outside of my grasp. For me, violence was the great equalizer, as I would see fear well up in the eyes of white America as I approached. I had reasoned that black men walked around like shadows of real men who were white. But finally, I was no longer Ellison's "invisible man." White America knew full well who I was…an angry black man, with no conscience, that had not made any acquaintance with the ideal of remorse. I was the reason white women clutched their purses, and white cops drew their guns first and asked questions later. I was a menace to society and America's nightmare all rolled into one, informed by the true doctrine of militancy and rebellion; nothing could stop me.

As I have matured academically, spiritually and emotionally, I have, at different junctures in my life made attempts to intuitively arrive at a rationale as to why I behaved as I did. It seems a universe away, but yet harkens to me as an old friend who is deceased but bares resemblance to a man in the grocery store. Am I that far removed by intellectual jousting and calendar years that violence is no longer proximate or a real entity in my repertoire of coping mechanisms? Were it feasible to avoid younger versions of myself in the windows of yesteryear, I would retort, "yes", but, my contact with such a life remains intimate. I have yielded to the adage of the homeland; that once one has been taught, he must return to the village, and teach them. My blackness has no price, and with this work, I barter nothing but the truth for its rightful place in literature and scholarship. I am hopeful that civilization might one day overtake the ghettos and housing projects of today, but it is not within the purpose of this America. So, violence must be. Violence must spill from the hands of black youth into mainstream white America from time to time, to escalate the volume of deafened cries of dehumanization, disenfranchisement and abject poverty.

I do not come bearing attractive words in order to romanticize violence, but to offer a perspective drenched in candor as rich and as vivid as the day when DuBois (1903) penned The Souls of Black Folk. Life beneath the "veil" insured that my pathway into manhood would not be illuminated, and promoted the belief that my upward mobility would necessitate it being instead littered with the bodies of my peers. I would have to crawl, scratch and bite to emerge from the pit created largely of my own volition. We (my generation) had always been taught, and a grave number of us believed that, according to statistical prophecy, there was no life for a black male beyond the age of twenty-two. On my 22nd birthday, I had finally ended the tail-spin of spending the previous three birthdays locked behind the steel bars of this country's penal institutions. I recall asking myself, "now what do I do?" I had lived my life on a day to day basis, with an immediacy, and in constant anticipation of death, fully aware that it was at my heels, and its' stench had pervaded my breathing, and then as quickly as it had all seemed to occur….nothing.

I began to conduct an introspection that still persists today. What was the incipience of this apathetic anger that knew no bounds? My rage was fueled by the fact that I knew that I had wasted good grades, and would never realize my dream of practicing law, and that given the right police officer and the wrong street, my life could be abbreviated, and no one would give a damn. Sure, my family would intermittently mourn and my friends would shake their heads and offer their fond memories, but whose life would change? My name would have probably appeared on someone's arm as a tattoo, but there is no time to stop dying in the "hood."

The cycle of Black Death is urgent and without pause. Killing and dying are so common betwixt these hues of dark skin that their occurrence is akin to the same dark silence as the last breath of so many in the Middle Passage. Our circumstance, our laws, our lives and deaths are meaningless to the world at large. I sometimes drift away to far away faces and wonder if kids like "Man" are still alive. Did he survive? What happened that our paths merged in childhood, and then so swiftly thrust us into different edges of existence? Did "Man" ever become a real man?

I daydream the same as when I was a child about saving Black America. Can anyone really do that? Would I yet be selected for martyrdom if I died at the hands of another black man? What becomes of a man that conducts a retrospective analysis of his quest for manhood and realizes that he has behaved like a child out of season? I have created more questions for myself than answers.

With every day that comes and goes, the genocide of black men by the hands of other black men makes my soul ache until I gasp for good clean air, partly because it is senseless, and partly because I know firsthand that it is senseless. I imagine sometimes that when I draw breath now, it doesn't taste like tears as it did when I was a boy. In this abyss of nothingness and pain every black boy wants desperately to be a man, but hasn't a clue of how to embark on such a journey. He wants respect but is deafly afraid of being disrespected. He is a warrior because, there is war being waged on the inside of him. He is the sum of all fears, things hoped for, but seldom seen; he is the manifestation of hurt, harm and danger, longing to belong and fitting in nowhere, at least nowhere that matters.

He is longing to become what God has purposed him to be. He is waiting to become a *butterfly*.

—

CHAPTER 2: THE ONLY LOVE I KNEW

"Why don't you stay with me tonight?" he asked with eyes reddened and a breathing tube feeding him oxygen. He was a shell of his former self, forcing a smile. His weather-beaten face tilted towards mine and he gently pulled me towards him. "No Buddy, I need to get back home", I offered. Then, he did something that he hadn't done since I was a small boy; he kissed me on the cheek and told me that he loved me. He didn't insist that I stay, and in my haste to be on the move, the most poignant moment of my life had slipped through my grasp.

I gathered my son and we scurried down the highway. We had traveled to a funeral for my great-grandmother, whom sadly, I had never laid eyes on until now. As shallow as it seems, it was a family reunion for us. Most of my family lived in northern Virginia, D.C. and Connecticut. As we prepared to travel back home, I saw a sign that indicated that my grandparents' hometown was only about twenty to thirty miles away. I asked my infant son, "Do you want to go see granddad?" He shook his little head in excitement, and moments later there we were.

My grandfather had been weakened by a triple-bypass surgery, but from all accounts, was recuperating on schedule and showing no ill-effects. My grandmother, who we affectionately called "Mama", met us at the door and immediately began trying to feed us, as she had done with expert precision and without effort since I could remember. There, on the couch, was my "Buddy", the strongest most compassionate man that I'd ever known. This was the man that taught me to ride a bicycle, to cut grass, to drive a car by the age of nine, and strangely enough to smile. My grandfather never met a stranger, nor did he ever allow a harsh word to fall from his lips during my lifetime. In my heart, he was my father.

As a child I would rush into his room with excitement, impatient to discover what adventure awaited us on that day. It didn't matter whether it was chopping wood or cooking meat skins in the huge black kettle in the backyard, I knew that I would be included, and that's all that mattered. There wasn't a trip made to the store where I wasn't in the front seat. Ironically, the brig where I would later be incarcerated was on the same military base where my grandfather drove trucks and had served honorably in the Army. Some days he would take me with him to the base, and shout to all of his friends, "I got my grandbaby wit' me today!" He would split his sandwich with me that my grandmother rose at 4:00 a.m. to fix. I never wanted to leave; I was loved and most of all, safe.

On those early mornings when I thought I might wake him, he was already out of bed. I recall being paralyzed with fear as a very young child, seeing my grandfather on his knees by his bedside. "Buddy, Buddy!" I exclaimed. Much to my chagrin, there was no answer. I shook his broad shoulders as hard as my little hands could. Something about his disposition comforted me, and I no longer sensed that my hero needed my help. Moments later, he grasped the mattress, and pulled himself slowly to his feet. "Are you alright Buddy?" I asked. "Yes, son...granddaddy was praying."

"What's praying?" I asked. "Praying is when you talk to the Maker son, and ya tell Him thank you for all He's done, and for waking you up to see another day" he replied. I remember thinking that my granddad must have had a lot to talk to God about because there he was, every single morning and night in that same spot for what seemed like hours. When I was unable to fight off slumber from my day's activities, somehow I always ended up tucked in my bed. I even began feigning sleep to see how it was that I was making it up the steps at night. Sure enough, my grandfather would carry me up, after hearing Mama say, "That boy done fell asleep down here again!" while laughing at my lost bout with the sandman. This was home for me; far away from my mother's screams for help.

Perhaps another reason that I saw my grandfather as being so strong and larger in physical stature than he really was stemmed from my father being on his best behavior when he and "Mama" came to visit; they would share the bedroom with my brother and I. There was a king sized bed with a white bedspread that we dove from our bunk beds onto, and also believed was an end zone after running the length of the hallway with a football in hand. When I was certain that my parents couldn't hear, I would tell my grandmother about the beatings my mother suffered at the hands of my father. She would assure me that everything would be okay, and that if need be, my grandfather always had "something in the car" if my mother really wanted to leave. I was too young to fully comprehend the allegiance and forced obligation that psychologically prevented my mother's departure to safety. It would ultimately drive us apart forever.

Every summer, I would make the voyage to my grandparents' house, where I was safe. I would cry as my mother pulled away in her grey Cutlass Oldsmobile, and I would weep just as bitterly when the summer ended, and I knew it was time to return home. During those summers, I seldom heard from my mother, and didn't want to hear from my father. At the most, he would interrupt my conversation with my mother to threaten me of the consequences of misbehaving and demand that I respond; "You hear me talking to you!" he'd shout. I would hold the phone away from my ear, until my mother resumed speaking. "Alright son, I'll see you soon." I wished my grandfather was my father so badly, that I began writing my name in school with his surname at the end of my own, and then later did away with my first name altogether because of what it meant to my father. I would write my newly contrived moniker on all of my assignments; an act that drew my father's ire even more, as well as warranted more bitter and one-sided confrontations.

I gathered how respected my grandfather was, by his neighbors, people at church, and even the community in nearby cities. I wanted to be a hard worker, a consistent presence in a child's life, and ultimately a person everybody liked, just like my Buddy. I surmise that this is why my incarceration in my teenage years would tear his heart into pieces. Each day that my grandfather returned from work, I would conclude my bike riding for the day, by chasing his green, now classic, Mustang into the dirt driveway, and tossing it aside to grab his lunch bag. "How was work today granddad?" I asked jumping up and down. My excitement could hardly be contained when Buddy arrived home from work. It was typically because I had spent the day outside creating my own measure of mischief, worrying my aging grandmother and was filled with boundless energy.

I suppose as well that the years chronicled herein would have been much worse had my grandparents not worked so diligently to dispense love to me that was sorely needed. I had begun the troublesome practice of setting fires and harming small animals like frogs and squirrels. I became enamored with the multi-colored flames, and never considered the actual harm that might be a consequence of my actions. Intrinsically, I was angry and had no outlet available to me to express my pain. Though it was never pointedly discussed, I believe my grandparents knew that I was indeed troubled, and required "special handling" and more constructive activities.

It was my grandfather that taught me the art of gardening. I would prefer to spend my summers helping him to shuck and silk corn than to be in the presence of my parents' endless squabbles. If the tire of my bicycle leaked, Buddy patched it. If the chain came off, Buddy repaired it. If it was ice cream I craved, Buddy made it from scratch. He seemingly knew how to do everything. I even helped him to change oil in the vehicles as a young boy. Little did I know that I was learning the skills and developing the independence that would be necessitated, only years later, as I struck out own my own.

I watched my grandfather give away produce that he toiled to sow in his garden. He drove to nearby cities to pick up young men and paid them for a day's work in the garden and about the yard. These were always tasks that he could easily do himself, but I got the sense that he was simply doing it to help them and their families. It was refreshing to see a family receive a huge bag of cucumbers, corn, squash and a few of his sweet watermelons, and the mother of one of those men break down in tears, following our pickup truck to the end of their dirt driveway still waiving and uttering "thanks". I think this is where I learned to be charitable, not only giving what one might spare, but giving a portion of your best. My grandfather taught me a great many of life's lessons without verbally instructing me.

Over the course of my childhood, my grandfather and I forged an unbreakable bond; he became my very best friend. Seldom was there a moment of inquisition that he didn't have an informed retort for, and never did I feel as though my presence was burdensome to his latter years. Conversely, I often felt that his love for me transcended that which he had for the children he bore. Hence, my mother and I were more like sister and brother than mother and son. In the country setting with my grandfather's male influence and my grandmother's nurturing, my mind could contemplate its inner workings and the gravitas of tomorrow's dreams. It was during my stay there that the incipience of my cognitive capacity was formulated and recognized. In a myriad of contexts and settings, I would demonstrate my potential for leadership as well as my intellectual prowess that seemingly outweighed the minute enumeration of my years of earth. Perhaps this was the true origin of Buddy's anguish at the actions taken in my teenage years.

I will never forget the pain and utter disappointment that filled his face, and how he aged right before me when he came to visit me in prison. The laugh lines that encircled his flawless smile were struggling to remain noticeable. The murder, that I was suspected of, was allegedly committed with guns I stole from his home. When Buddy sat across from me and asked me "why" over and over again, I felt as though I could sink through the floor and disappear. His eyes filled with tears and his mouth appeared dry as he forced the question from his gut time and time again. The one man that had ever showed me love and caring was now feeling like the life he poured so much into was over. I expeditiously terminated our visit on that day.

The reality of my whereabouts struck me that day. I would return to my maximum security cell feeling suicidal and as if nothing else mattered. I could see the weight of my transgressions bearing down on his person. While my grandfather had come bearing salutations and likely with intentions to jostle my spirits, he instead departed with his mental posture grotesquely disfigured. I'm certain that my grandfather did not envision such an ending when he continually asked me was I sure that I wanted to be a Marine. He had been there for every accomplishment in my life, and now I sat amid mire of such a proportion that I could not appreciate its breadth.

"Does Mama know where you are", I would ask when he came to visit. "No son. If she knew you were in here, it would kill her. She thinks I ran to the store." I could picture my grandmother worrying about him and his whereabouts, but thinking it odd that she hadn't heard from the young man she called "Son". I was even more disgusted with myself for having my grandfather lie to my grandmother, but I knew it was for the best. There's no way she could take seeing me handcuffed to myself, and shackled like a dog.

Buddy's eyes were yellowing and he looked peeked as though he hadn't been sleeping. One thing is for sure, I knew that he was definitely spending a little more time on the bedside than he used to. When I was finally released from the brig, my ordeal was just beginning. As I emerged from my cocoon, I would find myself again handcuffed by officers from yet another municipality. I would be sent to several jails on other charges to do even more time. Through it all my grandfather never faltered, and when all was said and done, took me to every city and township throughout the state to recoup my license because of tickets my co-defendant had gotten in my name during my incarceration. I would do another three months after this, awaiting trial on an old armed robbery charge.

As I bore witness to the distress and heartache I caused my best friend, I knew that I had to change, if not for myself, at least for him. I worked harder to prove to him that he was never wrong about me than I did to prove I was salvageable. When I got my undergraduate degree, Buddy and Mama asked me to participate in the ceremony; I refused. I seemingly felt that there was a goal beyond that. After all, this is what I was supposed to do, had I not deviated from the teachings of my stringent upbringing. I ultimately went on to pursue my Masters and half of the way through, I knew that I wanted to hold a Ph.D. My reasons had little to do with accomplishment, and more to do with proving something to my parents, and thereby turning my success into something punitive. I had custody of my son, and I'd mistakenly believed that my lot in life was turning.

I was doing well for myself, or at least I thought. After being released in 1994, I had gotten a degree, was working on a second, rearing my child and working in the mental health field. Needless to say, I was spread thin. However, when you've had time exacted from you by incarceration, each day you feel as though you are playing catch-up with the rest of the civilization, hence, I had little need of sleep. I was unable to sleep without the clanging doors of cells, or the marked pounding of feet that passed by iron cement cubicle. I, like many others, was fighting the inevitable mind state of institutionalism. Time became my prison upon being released. It restrained me more so than any other entity. It became increasingly difficult for me to get comfortable anywhere, or sit still for long. Subconsciously, I railed against having been sitting for so long inside of prison, and relished being able to move about without the approval of prison guards.

My visits to my grandparents' house became rare, although I spoke to them by phone regularly. I had no idea that my grandfather was having heart trouble. My mind traveled back to the false security born of my childhood. I believed that nothing could hurt my Buddy; he was Superman. The thought of him failing to recover NEVER crossed my mind. It was by sheer happenstance that my son and I ended up visiting him during this time. My grandmother would later reflect that there was nothing that could be done to make me relax or reside in one spot for long. She recognized that I had been caged, and its affects and their remnant were almost too much to bear.

As my son and I departed that evening to return to my new place of residence, nearly three hours away, after visiting with my grandfather, I had no feeling of dread or impending doom. Until this very day, those words ring in my head until tears leap headlong from the lids of my eyes; "Why don't you stay with me tonight?" "Why don't you stay with me tonight?" he whispered. At the moment I could not appreciate his feeble state, because of my own life's agenda. Why couldn't I stay? What was I thinking? Didn't I know that the phone would ring tomorrow and my best friend would be gone from me forever?

I received the call at work, and I could hardly breathe. I told my employer that I wouldn't be in for a while, and that my grandfather had passed, to which he callously commented, "How long do you need, it's not like it's a close relative!" I wanted to lash out and tear his body into little pieces as I had done so many of my victims before, but I was in a weakened stupor. I don't recall what I said, or that he (my boss) even mattered at the time. My world had just been ravished. In an instant I was alone in the world with the exception of Mama.

The guilt that I would carry, even until this day, was insurmountable. It felt like the heavens had fallen on my back and forced the last morsel of life from my being. I had never known grief like this. Sure I had seen people die, seen people shot, held the hand of a dying man and watched the light fade from his eyes, but this was different. Seemingly, everything that I had become and the pathway that I had chosen to resurrect my life were in vain. My grandfather had encouraged me to get a Ph.D. while in the hospital with my grandmother once. Their limited education prevented them from knowing what that was, how difficult it would be, and the specifics that it entailed, but it was a goal of mine, and true to form, they were unwaveringly supporting me once again. They saw the glow in my eyes when I spoke of it. It was the same way they had talked about the great beyond throughout the course of my life.

When my grandmother would lie in the hospice, clinging to the hope of proving the medicine of man wrong about her inevitability, I was realizing the dream of getting my doctorate. Under the tremendous weight of the misstep involving Buddy, I drove from the mountains of Blacksburg, Virginia to Duke Hospital in Durham daily. I was determined that my grandmother would not depart this life without me being by her side. I wanted to be there to hold her hand and make sure that when she arrived on the other side, that she could tell my grandfather how sorry I was. On her deathbed, she found a way to force from her lips words of wisdom, and a word of solace for my still aching heart. "Son, your granddaddy knew how much you loved him. He knew you were busy, and he loved you just like you were his very own." Again, I wept as a child.

My allegiance to my grandmother would not be rewarded in this lifetime. As my infant daughter and I returned to Virginia, I sat on the floor playing a video game to unwind from the grueling drive. The room went quiet and my future wife answered the phone. It was about one in the morning, and I found that I was among the ones to be called when my grandmother passed. "Mr. Lewis?" a soft and reassuring voice inquired of me on the other end. "Yes", I replied in an even gentler tone, knowing full-well why the phone had rung at such an hour. "Your mother passed a few moments ago, and she wasn't in any pain." "Okay, thank you" I replied. I collapsed over onto my side and released a gasp so deep that the earth quaked, because time had once again betrayed me, and death seemed to laugh at me with profound silence. I began to think that I was its angel.

My grandmother told me during the week that my grandfather died he had sent both her and my uncle to the PX (grocery store) on the nearby military base to get some essentials, and that during that week, he had slept apart from her for the first time in forty-seven years. She returned to find him biblically asleep. Coupled with his request for me to stay, I surmised that an angel had whispered to him that his time had come. A blood clot had moved up through his leg to his heart, after surviving the surgery. My admiration for his strength and protection of my grandmother, as he stared down death, humbled me to tears.

Death did not take my Buddy or my grandmother as much as it was they whom entered its rest. I was still bitter that my maturity had not prepared me to heed the signs, and time became my mortal enemy. Nothing prepared me to be without the two people whom I loved most. My uncle, who had been like an older brother to me, would follow my grandmother in death only months later. He was a mere forty-nine years of age, and another bitter irony found me on the phone with him the day prior to his expiration. I would pen a song days later, truly written to God in my angst that cited amongst its lyrics, "Pardon me, but I don't need another angel looking over me." In the song I wondered, what was it that I had done that all of the people I loved most were required to oversee my days. I knew the answer; my ethos wasn't strong enough to resist the call of death for my own life.

In those last days of my grandmother's life, I learned so much about living and loving. I learned a great deal about Buddy as she coasted down memory lane. Surrounded by pictures of the family she had single-handedly bound together with love, I held her shrinking hand, and sang to her as much as she desired. "Son, you always had a voice like a piccolo." We laughed as I cried on the inside. An unfathomable irony was taking place. In the depths of my mind, I could remember being a very small child, lying in my grandmother's arms, fighting to stay awake, as she sang and hummed to me in a natural wooden rocking chair; her distinctive smell of comfort, and her soft arms that felt as big brown pillows, until I could recall nothing else but awakening to the smell of breakfast cooking in black cast iron pans. My God, the universe was being inverted before my very eyes.

Depression and the strength of its embrace invaded the walls of my mind, and scribbled "killer" and "death angel" all over them in bright red letters. Why was everyone dying after they saw or talked to me? The answer eludes me today. I can find little commiseration at night. In the shadows of my heart,

I keep them alive by quoting their words of wisdom, and fighting to keep the promises I made them. From the days of those funerals, I have tried to force from my mouth the teachings of love. I have tried to remember to kneel at the bedside, never meet a stranger and bear the smile that Buddy wore. My heart fails me even as I write these words because I wasn't prepared. Buddy didn't tell me that he had to go, and "Mama" snuck off into the twilight. There are no words to adequately express the desperation and loneliness of heart that I have felt since they left me.

Time and I war endlessly, and I try to best it and its companion 'slumber'. I never let the sun go down without telling the ones that I love how I truly feel, and I know now, never to plan for tomorrow; trust me, it never comes. Not only were these the two people whom showed me genuine and altruistic kindness; they were in effect...the only love I ever knew.

CHAPTER 3: MA

No species can be birthed had it not had incipience of its own kind. In this sense, my mother, whom I affectionately called "Ma" was a butterfly. My mother was a caramel complexioned woman, with long flowing hair and a natural beauty that required no make-up. Her pointed nose was reflective of white ancestry from previous generations. She wore corrective lenses that were a rose color, matching her tone perfectly. She was fairly tall, standing about five foot nine, and by her own admission, was "a country girl". We often sat and laughed on the porch and joked. As I got older and began to ask of her more candid questions about life, and the circumstances under which I had been born, my calculative reasoning revealed that I was a "honeymoon baby". My mother had only attained the age of twenty when she was charged with my birthing and had to temporarily forego college.

We enjoyed the bond that every mother and son presumptively share. There was nothing that I could not share with "Ma". All of the courage that I mustered to go to school on a daily basis was exponentially reflected in her own life. Neither of us was permitted to have friends. Her whereabouts were constantly questioned, and I took particular note of how my mother was objectified and reduced to rubbish with a handful of unreasonably audible comments spewed from the mouth of my father.

In spite of it all, my mother summoned the strength to nurture my brother and I beneath her broken wings. I dreamt often of her death because of the abuse she suffered. I also secretly feared that she would abandon us along with my father. There were a great many years that I knew her atrocity, and that seemed to solidify our relationship even more. While physical battering enveloped our lives, I longed more for her freedom than my own. "Ma" seemed to be a delicate flower in the hand of a brute. She was proverbially trampled underfoot as blades of grass. Alternatively she was treated with the utmost respect in public, and engaged my father in the dramaturgy of being the "perfect wife." This, in my opinion, was the ultimate betrayal to self.

My father was a powerful man in his own right; educated and a member of an unspoken cognitive elite, if such a thing exists. My father was as charismatic as he was intelligent and possessed both speaking eloquence and a sharp wit. We often wondered how a woman so aesthetically beautiful would resolve herself to be with a man with which her attractiveness could not be compared. My mother was resolved to living in his shadow, and her attention was demanded. The years would pass and my mother would continuously lose her identity and sense of self, until she would be transposed into a trophy that was capable yet disavowed of an opinion. She was talked over, looked through and cast aside.

My mother was a nurse by profession, and undoubtedly was the recipient of her own most intimate care. What comfort could my small shoulders provide after my mother had been physically annihilated? At best, my mere presence amidst this quandary of survival assured her that she was not alone; broken we were, but still alive. One of the most morbid analyses that I inferred, was that my mother was dealt with in the same punitive manner that we were as children; seemingly as though she too were a child that needed discipline and correction. This observation would be a painful reality when we (my brother and I) "misbehaved".

Our world was centralized and restricted to our home. When we were permitted to go outside under my mother's watch, we were certain to be vigilant in looking out for the arrival of my father so as not to have my mother punished along with us. We would beg to be released intermittently from our cage, and "Ma" relented, much to her own chagrin. Our simply being outside posed a threat that we were oblivious to, but it enraged my father without parallel. The pounding of my heart when I heard the rattling of the engine in my father's pale blue Volkswagen, ushered in a fear that made my knees quake and prohibited me from making it back within the prison walls before the warden entered the front door. My mother was not crafty enough, due to her own terror, to contrive an excuse for our absence; not that any would suffice. We were frequently told, "If he catches you outside, you're on your own." Such utterances chilled me to my core, primarily because I nauseatingly discovered the shift in victimization; my mother had begun to identify with her abuser.

Why were we so controlled? What existed outside of those doors that could not find us as we were permitted to venture to school and work? What was my mother becoming? I had no fathomable paradigm from which I could rationalize the effects of abuse, for either myself or my mother. Saturday mornings when baking cookies and watching School House Rock carried the day, and times when "Ma" demonstrated her passion for music by chirping Dionne Warwick's, *I Know I'll Never Love This Way Again*, came increasingly few and far between. I can remember the sweet smell of tobacco that saturated the city of Durham's air, as I chartered the front seat to Kerr Drugs. As the words "objects in mirror are closer than they appear" were plastered across my mirrored image, I searched my face for what I too was losing; something was missing. I had not yet lived long enough to characterize or define what in fact it was, or comprehend the void that it would create in my tomorrows.

As I grew older, my mother's personhood was increasingly bartered for material trinkets. Every apology was accompanied by a dress, or shoes, and most consistently jewelry. As I neared my teenage years, my mother grew increasingly fond of these items; even more than she did her first born son. I deduce this to be the case because she cherished those damned things, and modeled them for relatives when they visited. I lashed out one day citing that each of them represented a beating that she had received at the hands of my father. I was ceremoniously banished to my room. My mother's closet and jewelry box were the symbolic keys to our prison.

At the exact same time of my rearing and my mother's battering, my aunt was amazingly undergoing similar treatment in the state of Texas. Ultimately, my aunt would escape her maltreatment and return to North Carolina, and even reside with us for a time. She unknowingly departed her hell to share in ours. My aunt, having taken drastic measures to leave her daily torture, seemed battle weary in her own right. She was in no position to assume my mother's emotional burden, and strategically avoided my parents' confrontations. As I began to grow in stature, my aunt instead turned to me and quietly chronicled the physical horrors bore in my absence. She called me into her bedroom one afternoon and whispered, "I heard 'them' arguing and she tried to call the police but he snatched the phone and hit her in the mouth with it and threw her down by her hair. There's blood all over the floor."

I choked back tears and at that moment began plotting his death seriously in the coming months. As opposed to being a fearful little boy now, I was beginning to acquire the physical stature required to bring a halt to our abuse. If nothing else, the defiance that I displayed with knife in hand, and persistent knock when I overheard trouble festering, served notice to my father that I needed to be considered. When the arguments began, my brother would look at me, as if to say "Please make it stop." Nothing nauseated me more than my mother seeking shelter for a half of a night's rest in one of our tiny beds sobbing. Almost instantaneously, there he would stand, a shadow in our doorway, much to our terror. My mind would project, "I hate you...I wish you were dead", as though he could hear it. When he moved himself from our door, I believed I had accomplished some small victory through telepathy. "We would definitely have our day" I thought. I fanaticized often of killing him; taking from him what he had pillaged of me....life.

Our polar existences would merge one afternoon in the kitchen. Before I knew it, I was atop my father, besting him, and forcing his body into the kitchen counter. Oh, how I had longed for this moment throughout all of my childhood, and then I felt a simultaneous tug on my shoulder and burning sensation in my chest. My mother was grabbing me, and shouting "stop it"; while at the same time, my father was biting me in my chest to repel my assault. I was confused. What the hell was she doing? I thought we understood that "he" was the enemy and that this day was a prerequisite for a semblance of self-restoration for us both.

A cognitive break had just occurred. This woman that I had cherished and defended with my life was no longer "Ma"; she was simply my mother. My mother's actions that day represented a treason that could never be undone. It was then that I was told to leave. There in my bowel existed a cauldron of hatred and a remnant of empathy; I was on my own now. As I gathered my things, my father's presence loomed, as if to insist that he was serious. I will never forget walking down the driveway, peering back at my mother, and seeing a look of something dying inside her eyes. After I was banished from the home, I would later attempt to subsidize my father's murder. It was but one of the callous and sadistic plans that I would hatch. I now had no regard for human life, and the love that had previously touched me and repressed my animalistic response to victimization, was dead. As I tried to resuscitate the relationship with my mother in my adulthood, she would ceremoniously hand the phone to "Him", as we had grown to refer to my father as.

My mother continuously tried to insinuate "Him" into our lives, whether it was by forging our names on Father's Day cards as children, or offering us up as sacrifices before him on the phone; "Here, here's your dad" she would timidly offer. In his usual gruff manner, I envisioned "Him" snatching the phone and mustering a reciprocal disdain in his belly as well. "Yeah" he would growl. Silence would persist but for a few seconds, until it became evident that it was a standoff. As the phone trailed off, I could hear "Him" in the background begrudgingly command, "If he can't speak to me, tell him not to call my house, and I mean it!" True to form, my mother would repeat the message as if I hadn't heard it myself. "He's still your father, no matter what has happened."

I desperately wanted to lump her with "the warden", but she was doing the life sentence that I would later be faced with while incarcerated. While inside, I continued to adhere to the cease and desist order regarding communication with her. She was no longer a princess that this young paladin was charged with saving. I was homeless and belonged nowhere. Her fate was sealed, and I had chosen to move on, or better yet, the choice was made for me. My heart was no longer fueled by disdain and hatred. I would try to put memories of "Ma" behind me. I did so by rationalizing that I really wasn't her child; that somehow I was adopted or there had been a mix-up at the hospital. This would explain why my father and I loathed each other and why "Ma" could breathe without me. In the film, "The Shawshank Redemption" Andy Dufresne comments, "Get busy living or get busy dying." I suspect my mother realized that her disposition entailed the two being inextricable.

CHAPTER 4: HIM

I suppose that the presentation of my biological father as an animate pronoun assists me in half-adjudicating a central figure in my development. It was as though during my childhood days, the mention of his actual name gave him human attributes. His treatment of us, myself, my younger brother and "Ma" didn't warrant that he be included among people with actual personalities. By all accounts, his dealings with us were violent, intimidating and inexplicable. It was as though we were a burden that he callously reminded us that we imposed onto his life. I have asked myself over and over, where such vile treatment originated from. When I had my answer, it still never seemed to rationalize the things that we would endure.

He was a dark-skinned weighty man, standing over six feet tall, bearing upon his shoulders what some would call a "presence"; the type of presence that commands a room. However, my brother and I recognized only fear and trepidation when "Him" entered. We were always on guard to duck an attempt to strike us.

We began to believe that we only existed to exact the revenge that he sorely wished to perpetuate against his own abusive father. We heard stories of how he and his siblings would be lined up against the wall, and have dress shoes thrown at them as a form of punishment. I presume that we were told such things so that we might feel privileged to be beaten with other less coarse objects. We were walked by in the hallways and brushed with disdain as though we didn't exist. As he drove us to school in his car, when he shifted the gears, if his hand touched us by pure happenstance, he wiped it off as if we were filthy little animals that disgusted "Him". There was not one day in our lives that we welcomed the sight of "Him". Painfully, the feeling was apparently mutual.

In our eyes, he was a tormentor, and a dark place in our existence. My brother and I would lie awake crying most nights, after one or both of us had been severely beaten, whispering how much we loathed and hated "Him". "He's your daddy" one of us would race to say, attributing this beast of a man to the other. I suppose we subconsciously knew or recognized that to have his blood course through our little veins increased the probability that we would repeat his cyclical discard for women and children. The words that would spew forth from my brother's mouth, served as a potential reality that I had not contemplated. Tearfully and with choking breaths, he said, "I ain't never having children." At that very instant, I asked of myself, whether or not we could ever be trusted to be parents, or if these horrors would be passed on to our children. I mean, that is what they say, isn't it? For the first time in my life, I considered the notion that we would be my father's victims for the rest of our lives. The pits of hollowness would reverberate with the sniffles of my younger brother. Sometimes he would crawl down into my bunk and we would cry ourselves to sleep. Those beatings psychologically separated us though; all of us...particularly from "Ma".

I war against those instances as a child when I, like other children, looked up to "Him". I would be remiss if I did not elucidate and expound on his stature as an intellectual and social giant and one of the most respected and well-liked men about town. As he walked in the calling of pastor, those were the times during which I felt most conflicted. He was a captivating orator and early on, I knew that the words he professed were the truth. My failure to see the conviction of his malfeasance that accompanied those marvelous words eventually drove me away from God for a time. "Are you going to preach the word like your dad?" people would often ask. I would smile an uneasy smile, and internally yell "He's not who you think he is!" That was the pattern of my childhood, smiling on the outside to conceal our plight, yet screaming on the inside. I felt nauseating guilt for admiring his gifting. In his absence, I would sneak into the hall closet and marvel at his priest's robes. I contemplated the power that was enmeshed in the velvet on the sleeves. On very rare occasions I would try one on, half afraid that he would detect that they had been tampered with, and emboldened by the meaning of the robes.

When you're small, the whole world and all of its inhabitants seem so much bigger than you. It was no different with "Him". He seemed to be a hulking figure in my world. I would always think of "Him" when I read Jack and the Beanstalk. I dreamed of escaping his hand every night. His shadow was immense and it strangled our beings on a daily basis. It pushed hope so far from our minds that when I would enter prison as a teenager, it was as though I had been thoroughly prepared for its rigors by "Him". Even the smell of his overuse of cologne created fearful pauses in my limbic system. Our maltreatment and devaluation would continue unchallenged and untreated for years.

Even as I scribe these words, I can seldom remember ever being told "I love you", or hugged. The hugs in our home came as comfort from being mutual victims. I can still envision the frowns and anger that situated themselves on his brow inside of that house. "Him" had the most peculiar habit of sleeping with his large bulging eyes open. In the few instances when we were not beaten within an inch of our lives, we were made to stand by his bedside on one leg, with arms outstretched for hours as "Him" slumbered. In our agony, we would look at each other, and when one of us would dare lower a leg or drop a limb, "Him" would startle us with a booming voice. "That's ten more minutes!" This only added to the terror, because it reiterated that we were always under his watchful eye. As we stood there in those contorted positions, I likened us to little scarecrows. We had no souls; they were being murdered.

We were seemingly at odds with "Him" from birth, as we shared nothing in common. In miniscule things we were opposed. "Ma", my brother and I were fans of the Dallas Cowboys, and "Him" was an avid Redskins fan. We rooted for UNC, and he cheered for Duke. Only during the times that his teams were victorious over ours was there engaging dialogue. Much to our chagrin if we protested his antagonizing too much, we were ceremoniously banished to our rooms for the ceremonial tears. Every interaction served to keep us in our "place". It was as though his every intent was to prevent us from enjoying our childhoods. On the one day when most children are made to feel special, and receive gifts that in their minds are paralleled with the amount of love their parents have for them, we were continually slighted. We would load up in the car by demand, make visit at the mall, and get clothes that "Ma" would be told to 'put under the tree'. My brother and I had no need to stay up late on Christmas Eve, or rise early on Christmas Day because we knew what our gifts were. "Ma's" modest salary couldn't provide us with the toys we sorely coveted, and with the maturity that we had gleaned from being beaten like men, we stopped asking for fear of making her feel worse.

I was reared in a time and demographic where it wasn't common to talk about "fathers"; this was more than alright with me. It was adults who continually prodded us regarding the "greatness" of my father. My brother and I entered hundreds of pacts regarding growing to behave purposely converse to my father. We despised that we even bore his features. Though I cannot speak for my brother in this instance, this is exactly the moment at which I began to hate myself. We would mimic "Him" when he was out of town at some speaking engagement. We would mock his scorn and mannerisms and find comedic value in his appearance. It was our passive aggressive retaliation against the million and one instances in which we were berated or disparaged about our looks. That laughter would ultimately become somber silence for me as I reflected on my connection to "Him". If I hated "Him", I was in essence saying that I hated half of myself.

My heart began to turn cold. With the exception of my grandparents, my attachments to people were fleeting. I had grown tired of screaming inside and talking back to people who didn't hear me, and didn't care. As I got older beneath my father's hand, I became increasingly bitter and violent. Fighting became a wonderful outlet for my rage. The more I fought the more proficient at violence I became. I started to enjoy harming people, and considered it training for the inevitable; a confrontation with "Him". I existed only in a half-hearted way. On the first real time that I believed I had found some measure of true love, I was the age of fifteen. I would soon learn that the attraction was born of mutual wounds, as she too was living as my mirror image. Her father was an abusive pastor, and our love was born of the hate and dejection that we felt. Ironically, we would emotionally cripple each other years later; perhaps it's all that we knew.

I tried with all desperation to hide myself beneath the weightiness of apathy and being nonchalant, but being "me" stung, and it showed forth from the inside out. I didn't take a particular interest in anything, because I didn't believe that I was good at anything; according to "Him" anyway. I wanted to be some other kid, any other kid, just not me, not born to this man. I couldn't escape my depressive state as a child, because no matter where I went or what I did, I failed to enjoy the moment, because I was cognizant that I would eventually have to return home. "What would I return to?" "Was 'Ma' harmed while I was away?" My mind turned as a carousel spinning madly out of control, with its patrons screaming; again on the inside.

I believe that "Him" could smell not only the fear in my heart with his looming presence, but also the disdain and abhorrence that welled up synonymous with my tears. I reached a point when I decided I would never cry or show weakness again. My psychological posture was hardening and the day hastened when "Him" and I would face off. There was no way to brace for the years ahead, nor a manner in which to deter what I was becoming. Contempt would turn to defiance for all authority, because I could not separate discipline and structure from the vileness of abuse. I started looking through people as opposed to at them. Every confrontation restored what was stripped from me at our house. I bear witness to the fact that "negative attention" in lieu of "no attention" is still attention, and so I destined to be an entity that "Him" would acknowledge in one way or another. My shoulders became more rigid during the passes in the hallway. I was slower to move when given directives. My greatest victory was finally looking "Him" in his bulging eyes. I wanted "Him" to feel the uncertainty that we felt, even if at a minuscule level. In the car, I put my book-bag between the gearshift and my leg. "I don't want you touching me either!" I railed on the inside. "Who cares what you think of me?"

I would say that I didn't care what he thought at least a million times over during the course of my life; but I did. I cared that "Him" didn't love me, or respect my personhood. I cared that nothing I did was ever good enough. I cared that everybody else's child was more important to "Him". I cared that I was never taught to be a man by the one whose responsibility it was. I cared that I would have no memories that other men have of fishing, shooting hoops, or fixing flat tires on bicycles with their FATHERS. I cared that both "Him" and "Ma" chose each other over me. I cared that every fight that I've fought in the physical and the spirit have been my own to fight all by myself. I've taken the scenic route to today because I didn't have guidance and nurturing. Father's Day is still a dread because I'm learning on the job. I was never adequately trained. When people remark today about my capacity as a father, I concede that I am the product of what I never had, and trying to be what "Him" wasn't.

I would reach out to "Him" as the years passed, only to be soundly rejected. There would be one moment in which we would make an attempt to bring closure to our hurts. My brothers and I met with "Him" to pour out our hearts, as my mother served as mediator. It ended in my brother having to be restrained, as "Him" refused, even in a conciliatory moment to give us the one thing we coveted most. He simply offered, "I don't recall all of that happening." It stoked a rage in us that could not be quelled. It was as though we were those same little scarecrows without souls standing aloof, without having our personhood considered.

As I pen this work, I have contemplated a thousand times over, what manner of atrocity could have possibly been carried out against "Him" by his father that determined him to carry on this cycle of uncaring and abuse, both mental and physical. In recent months, it has been disclosed that my grandfather was a pedophile that preyed upon a young child and tortured her existence with the birth of a child that would forever remind her of her rape. I quietly thought of "Him" and wondered if perhaps he knew of his father's diabolical encroachment, and was made to fear him much in the same manner as a boy.

As I began to investigate, I was assured that, for certain, my grandfather's wrath against my father was kindled the greatest among the nine known children. "Him" had a scar similar to my own, and as opposed to loving his seeds in an effort towards healing it, he had fallen victim to proverbially picking the sore. It had successfully festered into another generation. I reached out to "Him" as I scribed this book, only to be hurried off the phone, as I once did "Him" as a child. His voice was distant, cold and unknowing.

I felt the discomfort in the brevity of those seconds. I felt as though once again, I belonged to someone else; that even the truth of God's love, which we both profess to others openly, was absent in our call. The greater part of my existence shut a door, whose threshold it seemed too painful to ever attempt to breech again. "Him" was finally dead to me. His parting words were, "life is too short to deal with some stuff. I just try to do what I can while I'm here and move on." Was this a direct response to the news I shared with "Him" about his father and newly realized brother, or was it a cloaked punch set assail in my direction? Either way, I both knew and didn't know this man. In that moment in which we were both suspended, my father had successfully, and with some degree of finality, stolen two important things; my childhood and the hope of some grand apology. Amazingly enough it was "Him" that once commented to me, "hurting people, hurt people."

CHAPTER 5: DAMAGED

I lie awake now, even as I did as a child, unable to sleep. Memories pour over the face of my soul like rivers of frigid, murky waters until I wrest from this fallacy of rest. Flashes of the abuse that I suffered as a child visit me as would an unwelcome guest. My sub-consciousness is penetrated and pierced, until a frown accompanies the grinding of my teeth in my sleep. I am jostled by a cold feeling; not one of cool air dancing across a perspiring body. No, this is akin to the others. I flash back to the den area, and my father has just struck me in the back of my head with a fire poker. Whether the chill is born of shock or light-headedness I do not know. I do know that it is the companion of an anger waxed cold; contained in the small dark heart of a teenage boy that can no longer contain his desire to squeeze from his tormentor the last of his mocking breaths.

"What have I done? Why does he hate me so much? When will this end?" These are the inquiries that confounded my adolescent mind, bouncing aimlessly against my identity and manifesting themselves as single tear drops. It is a cruel cascade, for again, I am blindsided by a throbbing in my stomach that beckons me to remember hunger. This hunger has its roots entrenched deeply in fear and rebellion, and at times, a lack of sustenance. My brother and I would simply go to sleep hungry to avoid interacting with my father, leaving meager meals of "beans and weenies" on the stove; for above all we knew that violence was eminent without provocation. I could never truly taste my food as a boy, because one of us would inevitably be struck while sitting at the table and asked by my father, "Why are you sitting there looking stupid?" We simply preferred hunger. We were slapped or beaten until we cried, and beaten worse to "shut up". My mind struggles to find any good reason as to why our treatment was so heinous in nature.

Our lives were sheltered, as we were not permitted to go outside. My brother found solace in television and video games, while I escaped within the pages of books. I secretly absconded to castles with moats and was a prince saving damsels from peril. I spent a great amount of time staring from the window that had a taped over bullet hole in it. Of course, the curtains served as informants regarding my attempt to live beyond our prison and seemed unconcerned about the beatings we received. My mind wondered beyond hills and manhole covers, down train tracks into the homes of schoolmates. I dreamt about their lives and freedoms. I lived vicariously through their elaborate tales, all the while playing along as though I had shared a similar experience.

I would peer out of my window longing to go outside and play with other children. We were taught that they would somehow contaminate us and make us horrid little beings without morals. The only way that we could go outside was if my father wasn't home, or if we could recite bible verses. This proved to be an even lonelier experience, because often one of us would misquote our scripture, and the other would be forced to go outside and play alone. Moments later, either my brother or I would re-emerge at the door and sulk to our room. "What are you doing back in here?" he would yell. The answer was obvious; no one wanted to play alone. You tossed the football in the air, knowing that your sibling could not be a part of the fun, and was potentially in the bedroom crying and missing your company and thus, returned inside under the watchful eye of "the tormentor".

We looked out for each other like that. When one of us was being beaten for an inordinate amount of time, the other would appear as if to provoke his own or distract the beating from the other. No one knew the hurt that our tiny hearts felt, and likewise, no one could possibly understand the hatred that was being planted for harvest in our tomorrows. No matter what, my brother and I would have the bond of being trampled flowers that seldom needed to speak to understand that our fear and resentment of our father was mutual.

All at once, I am riveted again by the recollection of time my 4th grade teacher called my home, to say that she heard me use profanity at the bus stop. Nothing could have been further from the truth, but it seldom mattered. This particular adjudication was customary, so the offense, I had reckoned, mattered not. I was beaten until blood from my arms and buttocks trickled onto the white sheet in our bedroom. The belt would find my head, my forearms and any other body part that dared to impede this atrocity. I rushed to tell my mother in gathered quiet when she finally arrived home. She simply provided me with a bit of first aid and a look that I had grown nauseated with. The same hopelessness that chastised me doggedly had without fail crushed her personhood for more than a decade longer. There we were, two of his three victims, neither with the ability to reach the key, for we were but objects, to be broken at a whim and put back together again.

The amazing thing regarding the concept of fear is the utter paralysis that it causes. In my mind, I could but only make it to the front door to runaway. Where would I go? Surely, it would be worse upon my return! The guilt of leaving her and my brother to suffer alone pressed heavily against my frail chest, until I found it hard to restrain myself. I felt so weak, so alone and so desperate. This would be the introduction to the inclination to take my own life. It was with dread that I rose in the morning and with all expedience that I tried to close my eyes each night.

My sleep was often stabbed with screams of my mother being beaten nude in the next room. Each time that I ran to her rescue, I was hurled aside like laundry and told to "get back in the bed!" I would cover my ears with a cheap cotton pillow that was already saturated from sobbing. I soon developed the trick of listening to the radio with headphones on. It was then, that I fell in love with music. There seemed to always be a song on that soothed by aching being, and if but for a moment quelled my mother's screams. Perhaps, this is why I lie awake as an adult; they were never meant to be silenced. I felt like a coward, because I couldn't protect her. I later came to resent the fact that she didn't protect me by simply leaving. What did I know, I was but a child. I was often told that things were complicated, in hopes that it would satiate my pleas to leave.

On some days, I went to school with bruises on my body so hardened and dark, that I refused to dress for physical education class. I was embarrassed, particularly when other kids bragged that, "I don't get no whippings!" It's as if they were mocking me. Perhaps the signals of abuse were scribbled on my person. We received whippings for grades of "C", and were punished for "Bs". The only thing that granted us a reprieve was a mark of "A" (excellent). We would never hear the words, "I'm proud of you son" fall from his lips. Good grades were not an achievement in our home, but instead our responsibility. Hence, we were conditioned to attempt to be perfect in every way. I was ostracized, unbeknownst to my peers. During relay races, I envisioned that I could run and take flight like Superman, so I ran with all my might; the wind filling my jaws; the sun shooting rays past my ears. I swung my oblong head in defiance of my existence, but I could never run fast enough to take off. When the races were over, the reality of being bound made me pant even harder. Oh, how I dreaded going home.

One practice that my father would employ, that exacerbated the constant fear that my brother and I lived in, was to accumulate the beatings that we were to receive. "I just want you to know that's another one" he offered coldly. My mother would many times inform us of my father's impending arrival and we would play sleep to avoid the fulfillment of his dreaded promises. Inevitably, he always made good, and we were pummeled without regard for our humanity. In the dead of night, there it was, in the same fashion that pierced the daylight when we were too far from home to salvage ourselves from another beating; the eerie rattling of the Volkswagen engine. We would lie in our beds, physically shaking. Then we would count the tapping of his dress shoe heels as they ascended our five brick steps; then bile would rise in our throats as the key violently entered the lock, and then "Him" was home. I would pray a quick prayer that he had forgotten the beatings and would go into the bedroom directly across the hall; sometimes he did, and sometimes he didn't.

"Click", and then our light was on, and anxiety descended upon us as though we were prey. Suddenly we were being roused from our feigning of sleep by the sound of his belt buckle unfastening. Sometimes we were struck while beneath our covers, until we emerged to have our skin assume their place. My brother would scream the loudest, because he bore the greatest of my father's brunt. He would scurry to find cover underneath the big bed on the other side of the room, but there was no hiding. As usual, when I had been weakened by the thought of how much pain my brother had endured, I would step in front of the next swing of the belt. My father was more than happy to satisfy my desire to fall on my sword. It was as though he could read the defiance written in my heart, and was trying with all of his might to drive it out of me. We would grow to loathe each other's existence. My brother attempted coping by avoiding my father at all costs.

Even when my father raised his hand in an innocent gesture, we had become conditioned to duck to avoid being struck; for my younger brother, it became second nature. He would place his life at peril to avoid being hit. Often he was slapped at the table for the regular sin of "looking stupid" and disallowed to finish eating. As if he weren't moving fast enough, my father erupted from his seat and pursued him, adjusting his college class ring on his finger to administer an even more punishing blow. He swung, and whether or not he made full contact, I am uncertain of. What I do know is that the next sounds I heard sounded like the beating of a small drum, out of rhythm, that were accompanied by the screams of a little boy; my brother. He had fallen down the stairs landing at the bottom in a heap. A momentary dread flushed my father's face, and everything went silent. My mother rushed to the bottom step to administer her customary first aid, and nestled my brother close to her, screaming and crying. I thought to myself with sickened optimism, "Maybe he'll stop now. He almost killed one of us." There would be no such luck. The situation was spun as though it were my brother's fault; there was no end in sight for what we would witness. As we worked in the yard one day, we maintained a wood pile on the side of the house for the fireplace. It was my responsibility to chop the wood. Every swing of the axe filled me with euphoria, because it allowed me to act out the murder of my father. My brother drew the ire of my father for not completing a task, and was sent outside as I chopped. "What you doin' out here man?" I queried. "He told me to get a piece of wood off the pile" his eyes full of water. I was confused and cautiously followed him in. I peered through the den door and watched in horror as my brother was beaten with a log. I wanted to vomit and rescue him all in one fell swoop. How could he hate us so intensely? Were we someone else's children? My mind raced and paused in consecutive instances.

Our abuse was verbal as well. While we were never cussed at, we were characterized as being utter disappointments. We were always called "stupid" and constantly threatened. There was no respite for our fragile personalities during our formative years. My father managed single-handedly to make me believe that I was the most ignorant, unattractive and worthless piece of trash on earth. It is difficult for me to this day to characterize myself in terms of something positive. My mother was the weakest entity that I had ever witnessed. She cowered in my father's presence, and pleaded for her beatings to stop, just as she did ours. "That's enough!!!" she would shriek when I searched her face for intervention during my brother's beatings. "You shut up before I knock you out" he would threaten.

If she pressed the issue, her own beating was sure to follow. In my eyes, my mother was a relic to be admired for her aesthetic beauty, but hallowed of her substance and relegated to acquiescence by brute force. Perhaps even more stupefying to me was the reaction of the police, the community at-large and friends of his. The authorities cruised into our driveway when I escaped to summon them. When I saw the lights atop the cruisers, I felt as though it was a helicopter circling above the wreckage of my vessel. Sure I had battled the elements and the waves were brutal, but I had endured, and the cavalry had arrived! "What's going on?" one officer asked as he adjusted his gun belt and quelled the screeching operator from his radio. "Did you call us, son" he questioned. "Yes, sir I did", hoping to provoke the situation and demonstrate the courage my mother never did.

The policeman approached my father, and asked who he was. After a rather short exchange, the officer asked my mother if she thought we would be okay staying the night or if she needed to gather a few things. My father's eyes were defiantly aimed at my mother. What had he said to the officer? Why wasn't he in cuffs? I was too young to realize what the definition of "magistrate" was; but knew that it was my father's job title. The officer departed, and I learned that if I were to ever find refuge, it would not be achieved in this manner. At that very moment was born a great distrust for police, and I differentiated between policing and public safety. This experience would serve as the root of my disdain for authority.

There would be instances where we, too, would attempt to 'saddle the breeze and ride', but they were cut short by my father's apologies and my mother's spiritual obligation to "make things work". The years would continue with the same ebb and flow, each of us playing out our part in the "fit for Lifetime" story. We would find ourselves leaving for a motel when my father was away at work, but we always came back by coercion, most often through the persuasion embedded in some material gift. Even though the rooms were small and the meals originated from the vending machines, Ma's screams in the night had turned instead into muffled crying. "Was she hurting from this last ordeal, or did she miss him?" I tried to reason. When I would voice my opinion on leaving, Ma would yell at me sometimes, citing that I didn't understand how hard it would be trying to survive on our own. I didn't care; all I wanted was for the abuse to stop.

Outside of my father's obvious standing and influence in the criminal justice system, he was also an ordained minister and his ability to speak and profess the gospel found my mother both bound and smitten. My father was a man who was never at a loss for something intelligible to say; the world loved him, which made it increasingly difficult for anyone outside of our realm of domestic violence to believe the tales we escaped to tell. Wherever we went, people would recognize him and stop him for a dialogue, and we were conditioned to stand there and pose like puppets as he bragged on his "family".

I recall once getting physically sick of hearing the laudatory comments regarding my father's speaking prowess and how fortunate we should be to have him as a father and a husband, until I commented unknowingly, "Yeah, well you don't live with him!" My mother literally shoved me, hoping to get me out of earshot and smiled a painful grin, as if to beg the woman to ignore my utterance. It was too late. The woman ceremoniously told my father exactly what I said, and as we rode silently home from the church forty minutes away, I could sense the urgency in his driving to get me home and attempt to take my life. I was beaten that evening until I wanted to lose consciousness, but could not. This time, there would be no intervention by my mother; no first aid, nothing. I'd embarrassed them both and I had exposed our deepest horror. A line was drawn in the sand, and I began to believe "Ma" was on the other side of it.

I tried on so many occasions to find a soul that could empathize with what we were going through, with pleading eyes and mouth, but people either refused to believe that the good reverend could do such, or surmised that it was an issue best resolved by my parents. In the 9th grade we moved and I was transferred to a predominantly white school. This was my first time ever coming into contact with white people, and from all accounts I saw on television and from my readings, it was white women who could sympathize most with the plight of "poor black boys"; so I gambled on my homeroom teacher. She was a slim, authoritative woman, with long flowing blond hair, and often wore tie-die clothing to school, resembling someone from Woodstock. I sensed early on that I could trust her because of her gentle way with me when I remarked in class. I waited for the moment where she would but crack the door, and I would bare my soul to her.

My brother and I were beaten on one occasion where we had accumulated whippings my father had been tracking. Evidently, the number had reached a point at which they were massive and needed to be carried out. This beating was especially long and cruel. I would carry the physical markings for over three weeks. My mother, fearing that someone would see the bruises on my back and legs began having me sit in hot baths, presumably to heal my body quicker. As usual, I began making excuses as to why I couldn't dress for P.E., until my teacher asked that I not even come to the gym, but remain in my homeroom during my teacher's planning period. "What's really going on?" she would inquire. "Is there a hygiene problem that maybe you're embarrassed about?" The door had been opened. I asked if I could show her something, but didn't want to get into trouble. She stood in horror as I showed her the green, black and blue markings on my body. "Oh my God!" she screamed. "Come with me" she beckoned, leading me to the principal's office.

I would speak with the principal and answer questions. I would then be presented to the school liaison officer in preparation for a formal report. "Finally, he's going to jail for what he's done" I thought. At that very moment, I experienced something that only a person in the worst bondage could imagine; the smell of freedom. In an instant, it would be snatched from me as violently as a captured slave. "I know your father", the liaison officer said. "I've known him for years. He's a good man; I didn't know he had a son your age! What can I do for you?" he exclaimed. "Nothing" I quietly offered. "You sure?" he asked. "If nothing else, tell him I said hello, and if you ever need anything, don't hesitate to let me know." My soul had been murdered. The walls of the city had closed in on me, and there was nowhere I could run; nowhere.

There would be many nights when I would muffle my own screams of anger in my pillow, or lie there staring at the ceiling, with my ears full of tears that had sprinted down the sides of my face. My heart was beginning to callous and I would vow many times never to cry again. The scars of these abuses would haunt me far into my adult years, conspire to dismantle my interpersonal relationships, and torture my idle moments with the rhetorical question: "If my own parents hate me, then how can anybody else love me?" *I was damaged.*

CHAPTER 6: THE BRICKS

Ever since I can remember, I have been enamored with "project life" or the term of endearment chosen of the streets for the housing authority's residences, "the bricks". I am uncertain of whether or not it was the element of danger that pierced the air, the unspoken bond of knowing destitution defined this place, or whether it was the wanton disregard for anything outside of its parameters. The stench of dumpsters right outside the door, the absence of central air conditioning, the ever-present "cousins" (cockroaches), hard cement floors and the "love" that only the inhabitants can truly fathom, made the "bricks" a territory worth dying for. These "bricks" were regarded as the largest in the state of North Carolina because they stretched from one side of the small city clear to the other.

There were all sorts of characters in the "bricks". There were young girls walking to the corner store for penny candy holding babies on their hips incorrectly eerily playing "mama", double-dutching (jumping rope), playing hop-scotch or jack-rocks with shiny pomade and Vaseline accenting straightened but burnt hair and pink hot comb burns on little brown ears.

On the sidewalk, little boys dangerously rode bicycles far too big for them with a peer perilously seated atop the handlebars (being "pulled"). Occasionally there would be a crash that momentarily garnered our attention; one of the little boys that rode the huge ten-speed bicycle would land on the pavement awkwardly, and a "strawberry" (place where the skin was scraped) would emerge on his leg and head. He would untangle himself from the wreckage and run from the bicycle as though it had shot him. Moments later a young mother would come outside pulling him by his arm, with little sympathy, to retrieve the bike, swearing and telling him how she had told his "stupid tail" about the dangers of it.

On the porches were grandmothers with pitiful eyes, longing for the strength to climb down off of their porch to plant flowers and beautify their own little piece of the "bricks", grimacing every time profanity was spewed into the atmosphere by the foul mouths of children from a distant era of discipline. Then there was the old lady that sold "hard-cups" (frozen kool-aid in styrofoam cups) for ten cents; she kept a steady flow of traffic in and out of her door. "Clang" and "boing" were the sounds of her wooden screen door slamming and the jiggling of the thick coil spring that rushed us in and out to prevent being hit. Behind buildings in ponds of dirt, older boys played marbles and shot "7-11" (dice). Side bets often led to uneven skirmishes where someone's pride was taken by force.

Certainly not to be left out was the local wino, always a second from losing his balance, clutching spirits in his paper bag, as if the contents were a secret to everyone. "Come here" he would shout at children walking by or playing. He seemed to be demanding respect lost to him in his drunken stupor, almost as if we were supposed to know who he used to be. "I know your people!" he would slur as children mocked and eluded him. One of my fondest memories of the "bricks" was there seemed to always be someone who served as Saturday's disc jockey. Sweet melodies of rhythm and blues poured out of some hip dude's screen door onto the sidewalk like an elixir. The smoke of "special cigarettes" preceded a slim cat without a shirt emerging picking his afro, as if he were taking a bow for blessing us with the music. When he "shut it down" for the day inside, it was only to take his master blaster up to the "slab" (basketball court) while the brothers played ball. His stride was always relaxed and cool, making sure not to put too much pressure on his white Cons (Converse).

As Alexander O'Neal and Cherelle sang *Saturday Love*, and little girls danced in jelly sandals to Michael Jackson's *P.Y.T.*, I couldn't imagine feeling more free, and oblivious to the poverty inherent in the "bricks". We would run into my paternal grandmother's house and try to make sandwiches, only to realize that the "cousins" had beaten us to the bread. "Oh well", back outside to rustle up enough coins to visit the corner store to buy a a pack of Thiller Now and Laters, Alexander the Grapes, Pop Rocks, Lemonheads or the major purchase of a fifty cent dill pickle, which was carefully wrapped in tissue paper. Sharing a dill pickle with others required the practice of carefully placing one's thumb in a position that allowed a friend to take what the owner considered a reasonable bite. Sharing soda called for the similar art of pouring soda into the neck of a playmate to prevent their lips from touching the can, and reducing the loss of one precious drop. When it came to the newly released Salt & Vinegar chips, pinching the corner staved off being robbed of all of one's chips. This was all the sustenance we required to go back to work. Popping wheelies, ruining the girl's jump rope game, and chasing the ice cream truck until we were breathless for the mere chance to score nutty buddies and bomb pops was our job. There was no way that any of us wanted to be laid off or fired.

We did whatever it took to be considered brazen and garner the attention of those little shiny headed girls wearing far too much lip gloss. We knew there was no way to compete with the first two loves of every little girl's life; Michael Jackson and New Edition. Shag haircuts, waves, jheri curls, Member's Only jackets and Izod shirts would never cut it. The best a boy could hope for back then was 3rd place, and that was with light skin and good hair! Given that I could neither afford the material trappings, nor fit the description of what girls desired most, my low self-esteem was exacerbated.

Another symptom of the "bricks" was that they trapped heat at night. My uncles devised the method of placing fans in the windows backwards to pull the heat out. As everyone else slept, I usually sat awake and listened to the random gunshots or verbal disagreements that were the sounds of the "bricks" at night. I thought that the moon shone brighter on the bricks as a child, only to learn that it was the luminescence of the street lights attached to the buildings. There was plenty of violence to go around, even between my uncles and aunts. It was as though our little cubicle was training for going "out there". Our family had garnered a pretty good reputation, so I was seldom ever bothered up on the "slab", but rather looked at as an oddity because my clothes and shoes were different. I wonder if my love for the "bricks" was so profound because I could always leave and go home.

Some porches had a long white wooden bench near the door that could easily seat five to six people; ours was one of those units. In the evenings, when street lights would pop on, children's names would be yelled from doors, the aroma of collard greens or some pork product would emerge into the air, and kids would begin bailing for home. Kids seemed urgently reluctant to make their way; some stomped their feet as though nightfall had betrayed them, and some broke their necks, falling off of bicycles, trying to gather items that would definitely be lost forever by daylight, and getting that last forbidden tongue kiss. Our bench seemed to be the gathering spot for kids and teenagers that disregarded parental urgings for them to come home, and as we would find later, some tarried to prevent beatings and even molestation. We would "crack" (joke) on each other until someone's feelings were hurt and sing into the pitch darkness working to perfect our harmonies.

I probably would've stayed out all night on that porch enjoying the forbidden sounds, smells and sights of the "bricks" were it not for my grandmother gently reminding me of who my father was. Even in the company of my cousins, his presence was always a restraining force, to the extent that they did things and left me behind. "Boy, you know your daddy will kill you! We'll be back" they would shout. Grandma was a silent matriarch that seldom spoke unless it was something serious that needed to be refereed. I could tell by her eyes that she empathized with how controlling my father could be, because he spoke to her and behaved as though he was her husband. He too resented his father and battled him physically to protect his mother. It was when I was in the "bricks" that I understood my father more and more, even though I was reluctant to do so. I saw all of the things from which he fought so valiantly to escape. He was running from his past, and I was in the way. I understood his not wanting me to know him by way of the "bricks". This is where his savagery was born and his survivalist mentality originated.

Grandma however, seemed content to let me soak it all in and even have my first experience with courting. My aunt, who was only a few years my senior had several friends whom I lusted for, but knew that they were far from my romantic reach. One of them, nicknamed "Porky", (an oxymoron for a tall slender girl) had a younger sister my exact age, nicknamed "Pimp". "Pimp" took an immediate liking to me, and I to her. We blushed so hard until I thought my face would crack. She was far more endowed than the other girls her age in the "bricks". My mind had not even graduated to thoughts of what I might do if given half the chance. Of course, I had heard stories, but with my stringent upbringing, I was content to get my first kiss; a kiss that held me throughout the school year, until I could return the next summer.

No one could tell us that we weren't in love. My every thought was of her; not of her body, but her smile, of her being my "girlfriend". My aunt and cousins would tease me to tears. "Krumah's got a girlfriend!" they would chant over and over. It didn't bother me much after a while, because I knew "Pimp" loved me too. Her mom was a large portly dark-skinned woman that talked really loud and intimidated me. "You call yourself goin' with my little 'Pimp'", she ridiculed. "Yes ma'am" I choked forward. "Who yo' people?" she asked as she eye-balled me. "The Lewises" I replied. "Oh, I know all them", as she began to rattle off the names of all of my aunts, uncles and grandparents. "Okay then" she laughed, as if she knew this was a fleeting romance. Something bubbled up in me as if to say "You'll see; we'll last", because I loved Pimp enough to marry her right then and there at the ripe old age of thirteen. I, like every child at that age, couldn't be told anything. I had it all figured out. I had seen and done enough in thirteen years to take on a wife. I would treat her far better than "Him" ever treated "Ma". So, I did what any red-blooded

American boy would do. I went to the corner store and spent my hard cup money on a ring from the bubble gum machine! When I gave Pimp that ring, I presented it as if it was more grandiose than any gift imaginable. My cousins told me how she wore it with pride and honor despite it turning green during the school year. When I returned during the Christmas break, she was still wearing it. After years of living in the "bricks", my grandmother moved to a smaller unit and finally into a home purchased by my father and uncle. Grandma shed some light on something that I will never forget. Getting a house was a dream that she never thought she would realize, and to hear her tell it, it was more of her nine children's dream than her own. Grandma wasn't, by her own account, complacent, but instead focused on her home with God. That stuck with me for some reason. Grandma saw her share of family troubles and hard days in the "bricks", but in her I saw a woman that was truly content and could care less about money.

Thinking that I would never see "Pimp" again, I was surprised to find that she had moved around the corner with her grandmother. Life was different in this neighborhood; it seemed to be slower, but better somehow. We were able to visit one another and take brief walks without the jostle of the "bricks" and its nightlife. "Pimp" seemed different too. I could tell she missed her old element, and her siblings. That's what was meant earlier about the distance between the parameters of the "bricks" contrasted with the outside world. Not everyone longs to leave. To some, the world outside is too big to conceive of, and an awfully frightening reality; much more so than poverty.

I spent my early years seeing firsthand what life had to offer, but being deprived by my father. I decided to get a job at the age of fourteen washing dishes and busing tables in a seafood restaurant. It was primarily to buy myself things my father withheld from me, but as well to give "Pimp" nicer things in the summer and for Christmas. I gave her what I thought at the time to be a great Christmas, complete with clothes and a stuffed animal. She was so very grateful, and saddened too that she could not afford to get me anything. It never crossed my mind to expect anything. This was one of the only father and son moments that I recall with fondness; that my "dad" took me to the nearby mall to buy the gifts, and then to her grandmother's house to drop them off. "Him" was nowhere in sight. It would be the best Christmas of my childhood for the aforementioned reasons. It would also be my last with "Pimp".

As odd as it may sound, distance is not a reality until we come into the knowledge of its constraints. As teenagers, we didn't realize that we lived over one hundred odd miles apart. We never discussed calling or writing during the school year. Long distance calling was a luxury that neither of us could afford at the time. With that being said, our love dissipated and I never laid eyes on her again. Alzheimer's disease would claim the latter years of my grandmother's life, and there would be no real reason to visit the city again.

Little did I know that the aforementioned statement would be grossly inaccurate on two fronts. The bricks would be my haven when I was found to be without a place to call home, and the city where puppy love had its incipience would prove to be that place where God had determined that my self-destructive trajectory should come to a screeching halt. Poet Alfred, Lord Tennyson proffers "Tis better to have loved and lost, than never to have loved at all." I bitterly disagree, because the anguish of losing such fleeting bliss can never be satiated. At the age of fourteen, I would suffer one bitter breakup (Pimp), but later be reunited with another through bitterness (the bricks).

LARVAE STAGE

In the larvae stage, the caterpillar emerges from the egg and consumes the shell as a food source. The caterpillar spends an inordinate amount of its time in search of food and forms mutual associations with ants. The ants provide protection in exchange for honeydew secretions. The caterpillar communicates with the ants through vibrations and chemical signals. During this stage, a hardened cuticle rapidly develops. Needless to say, as a homeless teenager, there would be many nights where sustenance was lacking, and as I walked defiantly into the world of violence and criminality, I would develop much needed defense mechanisms and a pitiless posture of incontrollable rage and existentialism.

CHAPTER 7: HOMELESS

After the skirmish with "Him", I was punched again, not at his hands, but by the realities of having to survive. I'm certain that both of my parents thought that I would return humbled and begging for somewhere to reside; but I had been betrayed by my mother and thought to myself, that nothing could be worse than my previous predicament. My new teachers were "old heads", pimps, and pool hall characters. One such shady figure immediately took me under his wing, and I began selling heroin and powder cocaine out of the pool hall. When my cohorts from the housing projects were flagging down cars, and jockeying for positions on an over-populated street corner, I was in the comfort of a relatively warm, smoke-filled pool hall, utilizing the corner pockets for distribution. I soon became involved in pimping by default. I didn't have girls per say, but what I did have was a product that created a physiological dependence that I could only later come to understand as an academic.

Essentially, I had lived my life sheltered, whether it was in the tiny house, where all of my nightmares were birthed, or within the confines of the little chain-link fence that surrounded it. That fence unknowingly served as a precursor to my future confinement. It would also retard my street development and necessitate my having to earn street credibility. The world of illegal drug distribution was cold and unfeeling and my ascension to its upper echelon was predestined by my upbringing. I had essentially reached a point in my heart where I had determined that I had no use of tears and was willing to exact any penalty that the streets called for. I refused to be violated any further, subsequent to being "punked" by my father all of those years. I was, for all intensive purposes, Malcolm's reference to *The Hate That Hate Produced* (A 1959 documentary on the rise of Black Nationalist groups).

I had never been permitted to mingle with friends, and suppose that until this day it undergirds why the moniker has little value to me. I was an island unto myself as a child and I guess my father feared that we would be awakened to our oppression were we to interact with others. My father's mother lived in the state's largest housing projects down in the eastern part of North Carolina. Therefore, I had witnessed the ebb and flow of this lifestyle from the periphery.

Now, I was attempting to become a phoenix within its core. One way that I garnered respect was by acquiring handguns and then demonstrating that I had no fear of reprisal for using them. I was instructed to "shoot for the knees" if I was ever shorted on a deal. This practice sent a message to other dealers and addicts that I was not to be "tried". Further, it reduced the propensity of being charged with murder and left the offender with permanent evidence of my capacity for brutality.

Several physical altercations where I "blanked out" and nearly killed people spread my reputation throughout the "bricks". It also helped that I played basketball well. I was always sure to keep "heat" (a firearm) on the sidelines while I hooped just in case I found myself outnumbered. After all, no hood was my hood; I was an outsider trying to curry favor with its inhabitants. However, given our old acquaintance, the "bricks" just felt like home. I soon found that there were many other youth like myself, most of which had no father present in their lives. I didn't speak of mine, so my peers naturally assumed that I too, like them, was fatherless, and it felt good. We recognized our designation as "others", and affirmed each other based on the principles and values that we believed mattered.

My reputation for violence was soon coupled with having a good "face" or my word being good. I would overtly warn transgressors of the consequences of crossing me, as to set the stage for a grand performance. I placed myself in positions where my alternatives were fight or fight; there was no flight. I exacted, with fierce savagery, every promise to destroy and maim that I uttered. I would soon begin to claim some of the other boys with whom I hung out as my crew. We lived by unspoken, but shared rules. When there would exist no good reason to punitively deal with rivals that violated our sanctum, we voyaged beyond the "bricks" and discovered random victims. One of the most despicable memories I have as part of my clique was riding around some evenings shooting at people randomly. Many times I was roused from sleep at a cheap hotel or on the back seat of a car that I frequented to serve a drug fiend or by my pager going off. I would scurry to a pay phone and hear another mischievous voice whisper, "Yo, what you doin' man?" As if there were anything else to say, as I was typically up and about all night for lack of anywhere to call home, I responded, "Nothing, what about you?" This simple dialogue placed a great many lives and property at peril. The contract was signed with the customary, "Let's ride out then."

Seemingly, the worst encroachment against the clique was cowardice. More often than not, someone would introduce a dare of tremendous proportions to the group. One of our "craziest" members, Chicago, who was much more heartless than I, would accept without delay. Chicago stood about 5'10 and had slurred and lethargic speech that sounded as though his mouth were full of something. While we were the same dark tan complexion, he had freckles. He most often wore a confused look and never appeared angry, but was dangerous in the manner that a child is with a handgun; reckless. He and I became the closest of all the members in the clique because he too was an outsider, "walked in" (vouched for) by his cousin who soon left the clique because we had gotten "too crazy". Reportedly Chicago was on the run from a murder that he had committed back in his home state of Illinois.

We made a vow to each other outside of the clique due to my willingness to have his back in spite of only loosely knowing him. His cousin and I had attended school together, and my belief then was that any relative of yours is a relative of mine. It was the belief that I had no family that cared for me to this extent that led me to construct my own. We had all traveled to a neighboring city in a pack of about twenty deep for a football game. I'd recently had a run-in with police where we were arrested and booked because a member of the clique had three baggies of crack and a pistol under the passenger seat and refused to talk after we had driven through a random checkpoint. As we sat on the curb, taunted by the inquiries of the police, I felt helpless. I remember thinking, "I'm in this now...this is my life."

Subsequent to the game we all went to a local fast food restaurant where we met up with a few girls that we had come to know from the town. Chicago got into an altercation with one of the locals. As I was speaking with one of the girls, she said, "You'd better get your friend, that guy right there is crazy". I took offense because obviously she didn't realize who we were; when we traveled outside of the bricks. We were what people in the Triangle area (Raleigh, Durham and Chapel Hill) called Durhamites. I eased away from the girl and tried to resolve the conflict by yelling, "Let this sh*t ride homie. That's my cousin nigga. I just got out and I ain't trying to go back." One of the local guys scoffed as if I were lying. His disrespect was loud enough for it to create a momentary silence. In an instant, my face flushed with heat and I realized that I was in the midst of grandiose moment that the streets call the "spotlight".

I stood with the gravitas of the affront firmly on my brow, with a woman I was courting on the one hand, and on the other, the reputation of our city, our hood and my manhood heavily juxtaposed against my shoulders. I did what had come natural so many times prior to this night. I fixed my eyes firmly on their numbers, shoved the young lady to the side, chiding her to "Get outta here". "Wait right there muthaf*ckas" I warned. I went to the trunk of the car, and retrieved a twenty gauge sawed off shotgun that the clique passed around for "licks" (criminal activities), and that we had affectionately named "Rump Shaker". I felt the tug of the girl on my arm and her fading pleas to "Stop" and "Please don't". "Rump Shaker" pierced the clouds and vehicle glass to the tune of screeching tires that night. Philosophically, this was not a moment that salvaged my identity, but instead began to cement my legend as a "crazy muthaf*cka". The hood would hear of my exploits, and the clique would look at me with violent revelry.

Chicago and I soon began to take care of each other, because he too was homeless. We would hit licks both separately and together to help feed each other; clothes were not on the hierarchy of needs. The ones that we did own, would be washed at "some girl's house" when her mother wasn't home. We perfected the art of hoisting each other upon the other's shoulders to open the window above the door at the Heart of Durham Motel for a night's sleep, and would make sure we were out before the cleaning rounds, taking special care to leave the room undisturbed. That hotel was my lifeline and my new "serving spot". Junkies would meet me there to shoot their fix. It was at this juncture that I began questioning whether I had the stomach for this part of the lifestyle.

Chicago was still running with the clique to get "work" and frequenting the hood serving fiends at the top of the block. As the police would enter the hood, little kids on patrol would yell "Man down"! You could hear it cascade throughout the bricks as though it were someone yodeling in the Grand Canyon. All of the runners would throw their "packs" of crack cocaine down on the ground and kick them. "Come here you little prick! Is this yours?" they would ask. The level of buffoonery that the runners portrayed was hilarious. "Huh? What? What is that?" they mocked. It was always better to sacrifice a pack than to take a ride, in the white trash bag ties (plastic handcuffs) downtown. Due to the fact that Chicago and I were so close, I explained to him how crack was a nickel and dime hustle only because of the block's saturation. I was making seventy dollars while they were making twenty, with no competition. He couldn't believe it. A hit of "the lady" was $50, and was served with a $20 bag of powder for mixing.

"Damn" he exclaimed. I dealt with the prostitutes and their mates throughout the day. On one distinct instant, I would be forced to fight back my conscience and tears of disgust when I was asked to stay and serve in the hotel room. One of the prostitutes was a white chick whose husband was an addict. I treated them like humans as opposed to customers and frequently asked questions about the drug's affect and their practices to obtain the large amounts of cash they rendered daily. I will never forget this moment, because it would ultimately be the one that made me stop selling heroin. The wife had just returned from turning a trick, and begged Chicago and I not to move from in front of the pool hall. Of course, I began to get suspicious praying it wasn't a setup. We had fronted a pack to one of the regulars and beat him to within an inch of his life for not paying and thought that perhaps this might be a payback.

We stashed the packs until she returned. All of the while, the husband kept assuring us, that everything was everything. As we journeyed to the hotel, the husband began sweating and shaking profusely. I then realized what was happening; he was getting drug sick. We made it to the room and he immediately ran to the toilet and vomited. She had asked if a trick could come to the room, which really concerned Chicago and I. He broke into the room next door and waited with a piece just in case we had to shoot our way out. We were prepared to kill and or die to keep from going to jail that evening for selling "smack".

Inevitably the trick showed up, and he was so scruffy looking that we surmised that he couldn't be a cop. I examined his hands and nails prior to letting him enter the room. Chicago peered through the cheap curtain covering the sidelight panel next door brandishing the weapon. I gave him a "cut throat" motion to assure him I felt we were okay to do business. While the man was not a cop, he was staggering in size. He stood about 6'5 and was very muscular and "shiny black". While he was very meek, perhaps from the guilt of tricking, he posed a physical threat that I was unsure I could handle alone. Chicago made eye contact with me, and permitted me to relax, by giving me the reassuring glance of "having my back".

"Can you take care of my husband please!" she yelled. "Not without my dough" I replied. She turned to the large trick and beseeched him to pay me up front. He seemed leery of me as well. He then relented and gave me some crushed bills that he had stuffed in the pocket of his tight jeans. I could barely get the pack out my pocket before the husband began reaching. I repelled him with a stiff arm. "Chill the f*ck out man" I spat. "Hurry please" he croaked as tears ran down his drug-aged cheek. He got his works (needles, spoon, rubber strap, etc.) out, and I served him. I looked at him and inquired, "What the hell are you doing, go in the bathroom with that sh*t!" "There's not enough room in there." "I'm good right here" he shot back.

We stood in the mirror and I turned my head frequently as he futilely searched for veins between his toes, only to find one in his penis. The injection of that needle pierced my conscience as it simultaneously entered his flesh. I attempted to leave but I was paralyzed. As he shot up and groaned with the pleasure that sounded orgasmic, my attention was seized by screaming and a rhythmic smacking sound directly to my rear. The large trick had dropped his pants and was sexually pounding the fiend's wife. It sounded as though his nature was tearing her into shreds. This pounding went on for at least ten to fifteen minutes. I was petrified by the carnal fusion set in motion by my teenage hands. What was I doing? How had I become a major player in this moral turpitude?

The trick reached with long arms, and with one motion squeezed his pants back on, jostled himself a bit and exited the door without even looking over his shoulder. There in a heap, lay the wife of the fiend shaking and crying as if she had been raped. I tried to reason to myself that this was but a casualty of her profession, and I should remain despondent, but my stomach churned. Beside me stood the fiend physically capitulating, but never toppling, with a needle protruding from his penis. His eyes were glassy, his mouth was agape and he was unconscious to the world around him. A rage poured into my bloodstream. I grabbed the fiend by his filthy and discolored shirt and began to shake him violently. "How the f*ck can you let someone do that sh*t to your wife?" I commanded. I wrangled with him until both he and the needle hit the floor. I marched passed the sobbing prostitute out of the hotel door and as I recall, failed to speak for the rest of the evening. Chicago didn't press me and we crashed in his girlfriend's Ford LTD that night. There would be many nights spent sleeping in that car, and so many words that could not pass between my new brother and I.

When I told Chicago that I wanted out of the heroin game, he didn't question me. Instead, he shared that he had been making quite a nice living, without me, pulling "licks". Among our most prosperous licks were robberies and breaking and entering. The pawn shop purchased our spoils and would ultimately lead to our demise, as some owners actually wrote down the serial numbers from their possessions. The experience led me into the crack game; but this was short lived. We found ourselves robbed at gunpoint while sitting in a car trying to serve fiends.

In conjunction with unpredictable dangers such as these, I think often that the cruel anguish of being homeless was exacerbated by the fact that I was offered somewhere to stay, but ruined the opportunity to do so. My aunt allowed me to spend a few nights at her modest apartment, but returned home one day to find that Chicago and I had nearly filled an entire room with televisions, VCRs, camcorders and jewelry. "Lord!" she screamed from upstairs. "You gotta go." Not only had I allowed her place of residence to serve as a stash spot and endangered her, I had begun hotwiring her car at night and "pulling licks" with Chicago in it. We roamed the streets at night, finding trouble and victims at random. Whatever mischief we found, it was undoubtedly together.

On one occasion, Chicago and I were uncharacteristically apart, and two twins from a rival hood had caught me alone, and pulled a shotgun on me. They held it to my head and others from their crew circled me like a pack of wild animals. Seemingly, the twin holding the gun was becoming more emboldened. "You over here messing with my girl nigga?" When I attempted to retort, the butt of the shotgun grazed my head, and I was told to shut up. "Shoot him" someone yelled. The girlfriend emerged, and screamed, "I told you that's not him...I don't even know him." She then disappeared into the crowd and into what I assumed to be her mother's house crying. I was shoved and then the car was riddled with bullets. When I made my way back to the "bricks", I was in such a rage that I spat as I talked. I walked back and forth like a caged beast describing to the members of my set what had occurred; no one moved or spoke, intent on what I had to say.

It was customary for our leader to declare war on another hood, but I had been crossed. After two days of reconnaissance, we had the names of not only the twins, but their mother's address as well. She would beg me to spare the life of her sons, and utter that she had nothing to do with the things her boys did in the streets. It fell on deaf ears, as we filled her living room and couches with bullets, destroying everything that remotely contained glass; especially their pictures. I was hopeful that they would retaliate.

Much in the same way I truly did not want to harm her, the rules by which the clique lived entailed respecting "old folk" and even more, not harming kids. We were also chivalrous when possible. We simply had no regard for those in our age cohort. We once beat a crack head that brought us a beautiful Cadillac for a crack rental. Just as the clique was preparing to pile in, the leader of the clique jumped behind the steering wheel.

In a bold and unprecedented move, I said "Wait, wait, wait. Where did this muthaf*cka get a whip like this?" The leader of our clique searched my face to see if I was challenging his decision and then turned to the crack head and repeated my question. "Yeah nigga, where did you get a whip like this?" "It's my wife's car" he replied with an obvious trembling in his voice. I chimed in again over the leader's shoulder. "So where is she nigga?" "She's at choir rehearsal." Instantaneously we swarmed and issued him an official *ss whipping, finally relenting only to shove him back into the car. The leader then instructed, "Take this f*cking car back to the church and sit your *ss in the parking lot and wait for her!"

We had a strange sense of honor. The manner in which we treated children was the only other indication of our membership in the race of humans. When members of the clique had babies, the kids gravitated towards me, so I had an affinity for innocent little lives. I did the very best I could to prevent their eyes from sharing my horrors and protecting their innocence. I figured that my own demise was sure to quicken its pace and devour me sooner or later, and if a "lil one" (as we often called them) had half of a chance, I would ensure that he never placed his tiny feet in my prints.

I carved out a territory for serving crack heads. Occasionally I had to enforce the unwritten laws between hustler and customer, but crack heads were a waste of ammunition. We often delighted in trying to catch them when they ran, or simply smacking them around. They were low on the totem pole of humanity to us. In this particular hood I had begun speaking to a lady and her three kids. I dismissed her eye contact because of the guilt associated with my moral trespass in their neighborhood.

About a month into our conventional salutation, she approached me. I thought for certain that I would receive some speech about how I was bringing a negative element into the community and how she wished I would move on for the sake of her little ones. Conversely, she asked to become an intermittent customer, which in and of itself was an oxymoron. I obliged out of simple relief that our dialogue was far from what I had anticipated. Her once a week habit, expeditiously became two, then three and ultimately daily. Sometimes I would permit her to "slide" for a few hours of sleep on her couch. I even learned her kids' names and played catch football with her son while standing on the block.

She was what the hood called a functional crack head. She appeared to have a good job and a nice car. I began to notice the car missing on a regular basis, and saw her less frequently. I assumed that she was probably weaning herself from the habit or getting served somewhere else. Either way, I wasn't offended; I had plenty of customers. One afternoon, I saw her son outside and asked if he wanted to play catch. A fatigued look owned his small frame. He agreed and seemed to have a glimmer of light in his eyes upon seeing me; yet I could tell that something was awry. "I gotta get my ball" as he reached for my hand. As I entered the residence, his two sisters appeared disheveled and in a particular state of melancholy. "What's wrong ya'll?" I gently questioned. "Our mom hasn't been home in four days" she tendered. The mother had gone on a crack binge and abandoned the children.

I went to the corner store and got some bread and deli meat for sandwiches. I fed them for two days, and then asked a neighbor to call for help. I left the block that day because once again, I was certain that my actions had dictated that my personal soul salvation was now too far from reach. Chicago and I always seemed to encounter situations such as these, where those animalistic expressions of our own pain were held in check by a requirement for a hint of compassion. He never questioned my motives and actually practiced the same from time to time. When we hit a "major lick" as he called it, it was a standing tradition that he would find some old lady woefully telling the cashier to "Put that back", and pay for all of her groceries. He justified to me one day that it was like atonement for all of our wrongs. I understood whole-heartedly. We were two boys pillaging everything in our wake and needed desperately to realize our capacity for caring, even if we were all that we had. As an adult, a friend would comment to me that "Some people are just evil, placed on earth to raise hell with no souls." I guess we were trying to prove to ourselves that we weren't those people.

On a day to day basis, we lived with the conundrum of survival and immediate necessity, which was far from gratification. Our lifestyles were preparing us for prison. We didn't watch television or go to movies. We were becoming increasingly efficient and calculating with our violence. Our only considerations were where we would lay our heads, and how to get something to eat. Many times, old schoolmates would allow me to sneak through their windows and steal a meal and borrow their floor, but they often commented that they either didn't know Chicago, or he was far too dangerous. Most times, I refused the offer to stay because I didn't want to abandon my brother. As I began to bear this belief in my heart, we drifted away from the clique. They mistakenly thought that when we got arrested and returned to the hood that we had snitched. In fact what happened was the police had very little evidence because of our careful reconnaissance and planning those nights we slept and talked in the car. Who were we kidding? We were still "outsiders".

On one occasion to prove our allegiance to the clique, we were told that an apartment had been "scoped out" (watched closely), and there was a significant amount of foot traffic, which signified drug dealing. It was reported to us that the rival clique running the operation was heavily armed, but that the payoff would be tremendous. The only condition was that we were to go in unarmed. We never spoke a word, but in Chicago's eyes, I could see what was mirrored in my own; we were being sent on a suicide mission or set up.

In his usual drawl, he manned up as though nothing mattered, and slowly engaged me; "Let's ride" he said. I was unable to calculate the cost, because he had spoken so quickly. What was the value of a life that I had attempted to take on my own anyway, I thought. When darkness fell one night later, there we were, standing there at the door of a second level flat. I would not let him best me or feel the trepidation in my heartbeat, which was now ringing in my ears. Without notice, I banged on the door. As soon as the door was cracked, I put my head down and kicked as hard as I could. Seconds later, I heard gunshots. I was unable to tell who was shooting or where they were landing.

The rest of the clique had emerged from the car, and were rushing in behind us. I could have urinated right there in the apartment. Instead, we stumbled and knocked each other down retreating as the rest of the clique secured the spoils. I emerged unscathed once again. This would further exacerbate my belief that no matter what situation that I found myself in, I couldn't die. I was unsure if death was alluding me, or if God was protecting me. It was the first time that I had thought of Him in a while.

It was our courage that supplemented the respect of the clique within the city and out. We had established ourselves as a force to be reckoned with. Our mere presence became the smell of fear and intimidation wherever we treaded. As party-goers stood in lines at the club, when we appeared in the parking lot, people returned to their cars and "called it a night". We had put in "work", took all of the dares, shot at cops, rode for injustices against the hood, retaliated in the name of the clique, put in on bail for other members, and they never fully trusted us because we didn't live in the hood. We swore that we would never turn on each other. We no longer put in work separately; it was all for our common cause: us.

When we made our pact, I imagine subconsciously we understood that our lives were fleeting vapors, and that perhaps prison or even death might someday separate us. We were drawn to each other because of a survivalist mentality that could only be expressed in our world by animalistic violence. Even though we never said as much out loud, I think we both longed to be regular teenage boys and not little men. Life was hard and only getting more difficult to navigate. Those years were the most savage of my existence, and I bore abhorrence for myself quietly because I was perpetrating the same wanton violence of which I had once been the recipient. There were life lessons that I needed to learn, and the streets were the cruelest of all my teachers.

I transformed into something vile and unrecognizable. I would pass my parents in the street and not utter a word. Our eyes would lock momentarily, and then, nothing. I refused to look into a mirror, because I could not tolerate the beast that I was becoming. I was unfeeling, barbaric and relentless. In regards to the incarceration that was to come, while I would be wrongfully adjudicated, for my own sake, I would be rightfully caged. The only semblance of humanity that resided within me was the single seed planted by my grandparents. My circumstance would take care of the rest.

During that time on the street, nothing both humbled and emotionally disfigured me like being homeless and being transient. As we slumbered in those cars, hotels, residential work sites and the like, I heard the call of every insect in nature, the footstep of every living soul, the urgency of a crack head's knock on car glass, and knew the earth's darkness intimately…all because we were *homeless*.

CHAPTER 8: BY MY OWN HAND

"Pow"!!! In an instant there was a ringing in my ears, and I was deafened for a few minutes. I sat there in the empty room of my apartment holding my .38 admiring its power and its capacity for finality. It was a weapon that I had challenged several times; daring it to take my life as I looked into its barrel. This time, I'd flinched and moved my head. My roommate burst through the door and grabbed me crying; I was numb. I had no reaction to almost dying that night. I fail to recall what he said; I only remember his lips moving and him chiding me. "What are you doing?" Donnell yelled at me. This wasn't the first self-inflicted attempt on my life, nor would it be the last.

There are dozens of hypotheses and rationales that presuppose to explain suicidal ideation. I have found that only portions of them are plausible in my own case. Many argue that self-loathing, depression, or some mental defect is to blame for such an act that teeters between the fringes of being utterly selfish as well as spiritually unpardonable. Sigmund Freud speaks of the notion of thanatos, or as he calls it, the death drive. He cites that subconsciously there is an insatiable desire to return to the form of inert matter and the death drive allegedly compels humans to engage in risky and self-destructive acts that could lead to their own death.

On some days there is an inexplicable gravitational pull on my soul that seems to insatiably wrestle with my future in an instant where I possess no control. There are days and nights when the call of death is a romantic one, and the biblical sleep of which the scriptures speak calls seductively to my spirit that it is time to come home. The fruit of these desires can be found in painful memories, broken interpersonal and familial relationships, fear of failure and most of all a negative self-portrait. In retrospect, those family members left with numerous questions for the recently departed often cite having missed the signs and the pleas for help that tried so desperately to say that there was a void that could not be breached, an issue they believed to be ultimately greater than their own existence, a pain that no love could quell, an aching soul that felt torn completely asunder and an emptiness that echoes and reverberates until it quakes the mind.

There are those who purposely ignore the pleas for assistance as well. A great deal of individuals coldly offer that it is best to "call the bluff" of someone who speaks of suicide to see if they are truly sincere. The grief that accompanies such an insensitive and ill-advised methodology is unparalleled. Further, there are those that simply cannot fathom ever taking their own life. They are so far removed from such a response being part of their repertoire of coping mechanisms that they simply look upon the act and its actor, as foolish. Our lives and the measure of pain inside their days are definitively different though. There are also times when the actor visits the brink of death mistakenly and cannot withdraw the hand of fate.

When hearing of a suicide, I wonder was he/she pulled or did they step over of their own volition.

Having been emotionally banished from selling heroin and fatigued with the dangers inherent in selling crack, I began my life of selling powder cocaine. My career would have its incipience with small quantities stolen from the stash of my uncle by marriage. He would pay me to hold both money and drugs in large quantities. I would drive him around and make deposits in bank accounts that my aunt had no knowledge of. This was more than enough to afford my own small apartment. During my time in the complex, I'd begun hanging with some of the neighborhood teens that wanted "to be down". I would flash money and buy them Chinese food from the restaurant located right on the edge of the run-down apartment complex. I'd managed to secure a part-time "front job" at a pizza parlor to maintain some modicum of legitimacy; the aforementioned Donnell was the store manager.

My reputation preceded me, and I quickly rose to the top of the pecking order in the complex, after demonstrating that I not only carried guns, but was not afraid to use them. I had rented furniture from a business, and had decidedly refused to make payments after awhile. I avoided phone calls and collection notices often. One day as I entertained two females in the apartment, I heard banging on the door, and immediately ran to "my stash" to hide my uncle's coke in a plastered hole in the closet wall. One of the girls peeked through the blinds and remarked, "it's the furniture people coming to get they stuff back" giggling. I remember feeling flushed with heat and perspiration brought on by embarrassment.

I ran and retrieved my .38, and affixed the safety chain at the top of the door, as I heard my kitchen window crack. One of the workers was attempting to enter the window with a

crowbar, perhaps believing I wasn't home. I opened the door slightly and addressed him. As he tried to force his way in, I fired. Bang!!!! "Owwwwwwaaaaa" he yelped. The thuds that immediately followed were those of him rolling down the metal steps that led to my second floor apartment. "I can't believe you shot him!!! Oh my God, you're crazy!!!" the object of my affections cried out. I was frightened and emboldened all in one fell swoop.

Word of the shooting made it through the complex over the next couple of days. I left the apartment and camped out at my aunt and uncle's for about a week. When I returned, I was greeted with handshakes and admiration from the teens in the complex. "You wild boy!" one said. "I told yall, that nigga don't play" remarked Droop, whom I had attended school with. Droop and I favored a bit, and affectionately said we were cousins because of the striking resemblance and so many girls thinking so.

I began frequenting the apartments of the other boys, as well as at that of my play cousin and his girlfriend, who lived across the parking lot on the lower level now. We would play video games and joke most of the day without much to do until nighttime. As a matter of habit, I carried two guns with me at all times, largely because of a fixation I had with firearms. As we sat laughing and idle one day, someone pulled out a gun, and began pulling the trigger. "Watch it, somebody might get hurt nigga", my cousin's girlfriend shouted. "Yeah, go head with that sh*t!" Droop affirmed. "It ain't loaded" the youngster responded. I pulled out both of my guns, and joined in, "I know yall ain't scared of no gun."

Knowing which of the pistols was loaded; I put one beside my head and pulled the trigger. Click…and nervousness filled the room. This would be the induction of many to a game that would later turn deadly. It quickly became commonplace for us to assemble in one of the two apartments and play Sega. As if the games were not competitive enough, they were accompanied by braggadocio, threats and piercing jokes all to create and maintain the hierarchy of the medium-sized clique. Needless to say, guns were pulled and displayed as a show of force, as well as intimidation.

Two of the boys were brothers, separated by a year, but bearing so much resemblance in physical stature and looks that we called them twins. Russian-roulette found its way into our gatherings as a rite of passage. Click, click, click and then someone would realize that mathematically, something was bound to occur at that turn. We all laughed and poked fun at the one that ended the game, knowing that were it us further down the line in the passing of the pistol, we too might recapitulate. I always went first, and then once in the middle when someone else cowered. I honestly believed the gun would never betray me. I am uncertain as to where this confidence was espoused from and I never questioned my true desire to die, although it was quietly exacerbating.

An early morning drug run on behalf of my uncle found me missing the usual gathering. I didn't even venture back into my apartment, but instead went over to Droop's. His girlfriend stood outside with her head in her hands, tears streaming from her eyes and yelling "I told his dumb ass, I told his ass." I was puzzled and felt a bit of a start. "Don't go in there!" she screamed at me. Was it my cousin? I had to know. I ventured in, to see only two of the regulars remaining and pressed against the wall, as if they were being frisked. Sitting in a chair with half of his face hanging off was one of the "twins". "What happened?" I yelled with a fatherly tone. While my back was turned, one of them managed to utter, "we was playing like we always do." This was the first time that I had seen a real dead body and the carnage to what I was now a witness had attempted to force bile from my stomach into my throat. I stood there and watched as he gurgled blood and his eyes turned grey.

"Call an ambulance" I yelled with a hasty exit. "I can't get involved in this sh*t" I said posturing as though this was just one of those things that happened, and that I was bigger than the situation. The truth of the matter was that I was rattled to my core, and I felt worse for myself than I did the "twin". Not only did I blame myself, but I began replaying all of the times that I had held a gun to my head, or put one in my mouth, not quite realizing that what I had just seen might have easily been the outcome. Did I really want to die like that? Did it hurt? This would change the way that I engaged death in the years to come.

Years later, I was in a troubled relationship and a deep depression had descended upon me. I began to measure my life by the standards of others, and the pressure that I created within myself to measure up created anxiety. My eyes could but only behold hues of blacks and grays. I had a longing for nothing and I was becoming increasingly unsure of myself with every waking moment. All of a sudden everything went dark and silent. There was no life flashing before my eyes, no walking into a magnificent light or even the basic knowledge that I had lost consciousness. When I came to, a nurse was berating me and asking me how I could do something so foolish. Then I remembered... I had taken an entire bottle of pills in an attempt to kill myself. This wasn't the first time, and even lying there with a tube in my throat, I had reckoned that it would not be the last. My stomach throbbed from being pumped, and I cannot recall how I was found or who called an ambulance on my behalf. I do know that I had failed at yet one more thing.

She looked at me with such a countenance of disgust, and her look resonated in my heart, but for reasons that resided on two opposing ends of the continuum. "Have you done this before?" she urged. Unable to speak with the full force of who I was prior to this, and partly because I was parched with a tube in place, she retreated. "I'm going to count to three and then I need you to cough as I remove this tube" she offered again in a judgmental tone. As she moved to pull the tube from my throat, she noticed scars on my wrist that straddled and crossed my veins. "So, you have tried this before" she puffed. "I just don't see what's so bad that you would want to kill yourself!" she carried on. I thought to myself, "there is no possible way that you can make me feel any worse than I already do."

I had begun the practice of cutting myself to garner a release from the sorrow that was haunting my existence. I seemed to hurt everyone that pledged their care or concern, and I was an island unto myself. I ached internally and regardless of what anyone says, no one can fathom how intense nothingness feels. It is a sorrow that surpasses all rational understanding. My soul felt hallow and I could hear whispers of death calling to me in the daytime. I was doggedly tired and I always thought that if I could merely die, then I could finally rest. I languished beneath the weight of life, and regardless of how loud the laughter was; the wailing has always been louder. Death had never been something to dread for me, but instead something that was inevitable. Throughout my life I have walked headlong into its path. I had watched people die and I think even today that the dread associated with dying is magnified because of the grief felt by those left to mourn.

Growing up in church, the minister would often speak of a beautiful afterlife that we were unable to fathom in our wildest imagination. As a boy, I wondered to myself, why would I not want to go quickly and join God then?

I think it drastically important for people that suffer from suicidal ideation if I elaborate for a time on what it truly feels like. While I cannot speak on their behalf, I have come to find that the feelings that I have articulated are shared by others. So many people look upon us in judgment and remark how foolish we are to attempt suicide. There is nothing to be ashamed of. In fact, to have survived an attempt to bring cessation to such a complex and purposed entity is proof that our lives are not our own. I admit that I have been psychologically troubled throughout my life, but no amount of medication can truly remedy an ailing soul.

I think often that the pain and desperation that I describe is born of the uncertainty of situations and predicaments. Even in the midst of my rage, anger and confusion, I would often listen to radio sermons in search of some measure of spirituality. I once heard a pastor say that we go through life much like a child trying to assemble a puzzle without the top of the box, citing that God has it. What is so profound is that if we watch a child attempt such a feat without the top, we notice that he or she will ultimately become bothered, frustrated and perhaps even cry or throw some type of tantrum. All the while an adult stands idly by offering encouragement and gently intervening from time to time. Each time that I attempted suicide, I had reached a point where the puzzle had to be destroyed; the pieces cast to the floor or into the garbage. This is how I saw my life; an assemblage of frustration that could not be conquered and hence needed to be destroyed. Suicide for me was not about the value or diminished value, for that matter, of something precious, but an assemblage of failures and frustrations that needed to be met with cessation.

I had been ordered to counseling and been diagnosed with nearly everything behavioral diagnosis known to man, including anti-social personality disorder, post-traumatic stress disorder, intermittent explosive disorder and schizo-affective disorder with dissociative episodes. I have tried a myriad of psychotropic medications, sat in groups, and even attended individual therapy sessions. I affixed my reason for living on the shoulders of others and fell deeper into depression when they failed me. My periods of psychiatric euphoria drew others to me, because I was a walking party. I was loud, boisterous and aggressive. I was crying out, yet people drew entertainment value from my pain, so my cries fell on deaf ears.

Until this day, nothing bore so deeply into my flesh than to be labeled or dismissed as "crazy". I had heard the term in conjunction with my name so much that I actually began to believe that I was an unbridled force that there was no containment for. For me, being referred to as "crazy" was violently belittling and made me feel as though I were a small animal, and that feeling was one that I knew all too well at the hands of "Him". At first thought, I almost felt a sense of relief to hear from a professional that there was something awry beyond my control. I would later find an unparalleled solace in spirituality that banished the thought from my mind, and I refused to take another ounce of medication.

Medications made me so passively docile that I felt lifeless and time actually began to move slower. This was a peculiar brand of torture because everything seemed to be dragging and my mind functioned at a rate faster than my body could react. For instance, someone might say something to me for which I would usually become violent and it was as though I existed outside of myself witnessing the interaction. My mind would say to me, "what are you waiting for, punch him in the mouth?" My body however, refused to comply, and I would find myself angry after the person had left my presence.

I was quickly irritated with the patronizing of psychiatrists and psychologists. I found myself being pampered and petted as though I were some beast that needed to be handled. My cognition had only suffered in the areas of memory loss. "Where have you been?" my boss would ask. "I got lost" I responded. There would be days upon which I began losing time when I was driving. I was headed to work and ended up in another city an hour and a half away. I would lose things, like keys, documents and forget what I was going into the next room to do. This frustrated me to no end, and I would become belligerent and destroy things. When I was agitated I noticed that I would become flustered and begin sweating. The only thing that quenched my anger was the destruction of an individual or inanimate object. I have broken my fingers and knuckles countless times. If I had a dollar for every window I broke or every wall I punched through, money would be a matter of frivolity. I would often go on profanity-laced tirades, feeling some sense of relief for berating or hurting other people or things, just so long as the hatred didn't reside with me; I couldn't handle it.

I try to recall the first time that I felt that suicide was not only a viable option, but the only response remaining in my repertoire of coping mechanisms. I tried to hang myself when I was thirteen because my mother told me that I was a mistake. She maintains to this day that she didn't mean it, yet it was as though I needed to believe that I was because it would substantiate what I felt about myself. I've reckoned that self-loathing is advanced weaponry that perverts our perspective.

As someone that struggles with self-esteem issues, I've always managed to turn a compliment into an assault by rationalizing that an ulterior motive was embedded within it.

The willingness to take my own life and assassinate my purpose had such an alarming depth to it that to simply say that I was depressed would be a mischaracterization of the root cause of my self-derogation. It was as though this process that we call life had chosen to punish me, turned me inside out for all of my pain to be shown to the world and my hands restrained figuratively behind my back. The most loathsome part of it was that I suffered in silence and in accompanied isolation. Who could I possibly utter a word to regarding my feelings? I would become a social pariah and an outcast. Thoughts of suicide are a private hell because its' discussion has historically been taboo.

I remember a guy that played ball with us at a local gym. Several successive times that we gathered to play, he didn't show, and because he was not prolific at playing, his absence had not been particularly alarming to anyone. I remember asking about him, and one of the regulars replied, "Oh you didn't hear? He killed himself...dumb ass shot himself over a girl." In that instant I mourned him silently and imagined that I knew exactly the thoughts barreling through his mind when he pulled the trigger. One more thing resonated with me though; the apathy with which his death was reported to me and the manner in which his suicide had been adjudicated as irrational. There was no moment of silence at the gym, no news report; nothing. I imagine that this girl was all he believed that he had in this world and that if he ever shared his despair over her, he would be called "stupid."

The fact of the matter is that for those who struggle with suicidal thoughts, the scales are tilted towards dying as opposed to living and it feels as though no one can possibly understand how aggrandized life's problems appear from your perspective. Many times, there seems to be a series of negative events that occur in succession and the pain refuses to relent, as it consumes the core life force within you. At a moment's notice, you become fatigued; your eyes are flushed with tears that singe your being, your heart beats ever so methodically in your ears, swallowing becomes increasingly difficult, and all you want at that instant is to be free of an indescribable misery. The faces of those you love the most began to appear, and you release each one inside of a tear as it streams to the corner of your mouth. Thoughts of whether or not you will be forgiven and the pain that your dying will cause others becomes muted by recollections of cries that went ignored.

The brink of fatality is a sterile place; silent, lonely and cold. The silence and peace of what death might be like would attempt to entice my mind to the edge of a cliff and looking over seemed as though it were an inviting place of solace. It is the outstretched arms of the soul standing in that place with a breeze that isn't violent, but dries the eyes, prickles the flesh and utters softly that it's okay to give up. I have been lulled so deeply into apathy, thoughts of failure, and not mattering that I have sometimes felt that suicide was my dutiful necessity. I recall walking in the mall aimlessly from store to store and feeling the urge to leap over the rail from the third floor. I was numbed by the inclination to do so.

I am so graciously thankful that the hands of time and death conspired with my destiny and resolved that my conscience needed to be consulted. Such a meeting makes us consider that there is a possibility, no matter how slight, that things can get better. All at once, the edge of the cliff becomes a frightening place, and the soul drops to its knees and clings to the soil beneath. "I almost did it this time. What was I thinking?" Slowly, the will to live inches back and only the remnant of shame remains, stuffed into the closets of the mind, never to be spoken of…until now.

During my periods of mental sobriety, I realize that I have allowed myself to be measured in terms of superlatives and not relativity. In my opinion, the pressure, regardless of the source, to be the very best at something sets the stage for massive disappointment. A myriad of factors beyond our control increase the propensity for falling short. Tiny battles rage within the most competitive of us and the mounting desire to attain lofty goals many times lead to anger, rage and overall unpleasantness. No one wants to be regarded as a "loser", because it overtly confirms the negative self-portrait that takes up residence in the subconscious of an individual that suffers from low self-esteem or self-doubting. I have always marveled at graceful losers, for they are an oddity to me. Simultaneously, they are seemingly the people most at peace.

I have survived my own hand by coming to understand that if I can withstand my trials that things will inevitably get better. Each time that I have bowed and been defeated by life, I have been blessed enough to witness a resolution and in many cases good fortune of which I was undeserving. I have always struggled with the notion of not giving power to situations by crumbling in the face of contrived adversity. As many times as I have had to stand with the winds of life pummeling my face and scarring my identity, I now realize that I have inevitably been molded into a person of great worth by life's treacherous weather. If I can offer but one word of encouragement, it would be to say that you are not alone in the thoughts that you've had. I would survive my own hand on numerous occasions; walk away from two near fatal automobile crashes where the cars were totaled but I was not even injured, shot at from point blank range on three occasions and spared a life in prison. After hearing my story, one of my mentors simply commented, *"you cannot kill that which is destined to live."*

PUPA STAGE

The pupa stage is commonly referred to as the resting or transitional stage. While the caterpillar is full-grown at this point, it has stopped eating and dependent on its species, it may be found resting suspended underneath a branch or even buried in leaves underground. While the pupa stage typically ranges from a few weeks to a month in duration, some species have pupa stages where time in the cocoon lasts up to two years. The cells that are developing inside of the protective cocoon make adult life as a butterfly possible. Marine Corps boot camp, a very brief stint in the military and the state's penal institutions would serve as my cocoon. I would consume the life lessons necessary to make it to the next stage. While in the midst of a storm all that one truly desires is to be out of its eye, for the rain to stop, and for the clouds to move away as quickly as they appeared. However, if we move in haste and simply out of discomfort, we fail to appreciate the rainbow that is to come.

CHAPTER 9: I'M A SOLDIER

"Are you sure you want to do this nephew?" my uncle by marriage persisted about my announcement to stop hustling and join the military. "I gotta be my own man and the Marines will help me do that" I rationalized. He and I had developed a "business relationship" where he served as my primary powder cocaine supplier. As a teenager I handled inordinate amounts of cash and stashed "product" for him at my unfurnished hovel. "Never keep your stash where you lay your head nephew!" was one the lessons he always infused. "Boy, your aunt would kill me if she knew I had you involved in this sh*t." His words had fallen on deaf ears. The worry of being robbed, shorted or even killed had exacerbated my sense of paranoia, and fatigued me, literally. In addition, I was reeled in by a large signing bonus and the knowledge that the Marine Corps would carefully instruct me on how to be the hard bodied killer with the flinching jaw line, wearing dress blues as seen in those recruitment commercials. I wanted to be rugged and unflinching, and of course, subconsciously one of a few good men.

I departed to n e a r b y Raleigh to be sworn in, and the next few months of my life would intersect with the misguided anger of my past to construct one of the most callous personalities encased in flesh. We were dealt with harshly, stripped of our individuality and force fed the philosophy that we were part of a machine, that there was no concept of race; we were all green. We were to stand in service of the greatest nation on earth and defend her freedom with our very lives; nothing less would be accepted. I would return to the civilian world with the belief that I was indestructible, impenetrable and an immovable object devoid of human frailty. One particular story that pulled me in regarded how the Germans had witnessed the ferociousness with which Marines fought in WWII and attributed them the name teufel huden, which is interpreted "Dogs from Hell". I was sold from that point on; I was a devil dog.

"Wake up, wake up, wake up!" Clang, clang, clang! "Get out of the rack, get on line!" We were often kept up most of the evening and then awakened by the sound of a trashcan being banged, which echoed horribly through the squad bay. Intermittently someone would rush to the line where we were to be counted half awake, and fall straight back banging their head against our wooden footlockers. We existed at the whim of drill instructors. Some nights, after we had behaved like true "recruits" for the Marine Corps, we would believe that surely a day had come when we would be treated humanely, only to have all of our combination locks locked together, tossed to the end of the squad bay and given a short time to figure out which one belonged to us. Our daily regiment included exercise, exercise and more exercise.

I quickly drew the attention of one drill instructor who insured that my weeks on Parris Island would be longer and more tumultuous than any of the other recruits. "Lewis! Get over here boy!" He would spend every moment making me run to him and run back to get information. If I displayed an attitude or moved too slow, it was much to the chagrin of the entire platoon as they were forced to "dig" (do sit ups and pushups in a large sand box) as I looked on. "Everybody say thank you Lewis", he would direct them. "Thank you Lewis" the platoon would shout, and all of a sudden, I was an outcast again. One of the most painful experiences that I've ever had was on that island. We were forced to get up and battle sand fleas. As we stood in the chow line, it was common to see a recruit quickly smack himself half silly as the sand fleas tore at his flesh. "Let my bugs eat!" a drill instructor would bark. Any movement that was not the result of a directive warranted the presence of as many drill instructors as were available parked in your face, yelling obscenities and quoting how undisciplined you were, and that you were an insult to this man's Marine Corps!

My coping medium about half of the way through boot camp became apathy that shown through to my face as a smirk. Needless to say this was not welcomed behavior, and I was soon identified to all passersby as the "nastiest recruit" or "an undisciplined nasty little thing." The more I was verbally attacked and demeaned the funnier it became because I wasn't breaking. It worked on more of us than it failed to. One recruit in particular garnered more attention than even I did. The stress of the entire process, having your head shaved, being driven to a remote location, keeping inhumane hours, being barked at constantly, having no contact with the outside world, and being physically taken to task and pushed beyond your wildest dreams took its own pint of blood. This guy began urinating in his rack (bunk), and we were assigned to change it every morning at reveille, as he stood sucking his thumb.

We began to dig as a platoon so much because of this recruit that the drill instructors seemed to forget about me a bit, and I was able to focus on acquiring the skills of a good recruit; performing well at the rifle range, in hand-to-hand combat, boxing, and navigation. The platoon had all but turned on the recruit and began beating him during fire watch (shifts where recruits patrolled the squad bay at night) with soap. True to form, he would cry himself to sleep and wet his bunk again and again. When we attended the rifle range, the recruit jumped to his feet and walked right in front of us as we were firing! Every drill instructor, from every platoon, from every company surrounded the kid and berated him until it sounded and looked like a swarm of bees. Later that evening, his effects were inspected and he was found to be in possession of a live round of ammunition. Even though I could fully identify with his pain on multiple levels, I could not extend my hand to him for some reason.

Coupled with the seriousness of this incident and the rapid approaching of graduation, the drill instructors eased up a tiny bit, and we began to feel like soldiers. Moreover, I was achieving exactly what I had hoped; I was becoming efficient at fatalistic violence, which in my mind qualified me as a man. With every pushup, pull-up and grueling task, I envisioned my father. I had made up in my mind that he would die by my hands as soon as I returned home from boot camp. I became meaner and stronger with every passing day. Every aspect of my training gave me physical and mental fortitude that I never imagined was possible after so many years of being abused and cast aside. I was more focused than ever. While my fellow recruits were preparing for the potentiality of being sent to Desert Storm, I knew exactly where my enemy was.

My senior drill instructor was a very dark skinned man with an almost humped over muscular and thin frame. He had a large pointed nose, very white teeth, and a booming voice. He was a very intimidating presence. Staff Sergeant Rush's biceps bulged from his elongated arms that seemed disproportionate to his body. In the middle of the night, he roused me from my bunk and asked that I come into his office. I had written a letter to my mother in language that articulated both my disdain for the swamp of South Carolina and the drill instructor's bugs, but mostly my father. Both her letter and mine had been read by the authorities at Parris Island. The senior drill instructor probed my mind seemingly to see if I was fit to continue training. It was a side of him that I'd never seen. He was compassionate and soft-spoken, and chastened me that my intentions were misguided and that my focus needed to turn from hatred to training to be a soldier. Unbeknownst to either of us, I would need this training for basic survival.

I graduated from boot camp and it was my parents who came to pick me up as opposed to my grandparents whom I wanted there. My father and I glared at each other. My skin had darkened and my body had hardened from the sun on the parade deck in the swamp. I was clean shaven, bald-headed and stood at attention without order. My body was rigid, and I recall my mother saying "relax son." I replied, "I'm fine ma'am". I could tell that my father was uneasy. "What have they done to you? Is this what they teach you, to behave like a robot?" Again I replied in short order "It's called discipline ma'am."

I would have one week of respite before I was to report to Marine Combat Training. The first night that I got home, I saw a high school classmate that began taunting me. "You think you a big man now huh nigga?" We had been very close friends, and it was now evident that he was bitter about my departure, not to mention an unresolved incident regarding a particular young lady he fancied. "I bet you won't try me", I invited. He leapt from the convertible car he was sitting in, and my next recollection was of me stomping him as he lay with his head pinned near the front car tire. Along with the last kick, I spat on him. This new level of rage was intoxicating. I was capable of swift and personal justice for what I considered an affront. My father was next.

I stayed at my parents' house waiting for my week to expire. I hated being there. There were so many memories; the beatings, the fights; being thrown out. My brothers were like little strangers to me. They barely recognized my new demeanor. I had to get out of the house. I went to my aunt's apartment, which had been my place of refuge and called around until I found Chicago who welcomed me back with open arms. He transported me all over the city and we reminisced about what seemed like years ago. I told him how I had to stomp out an old classmate; "Niggas tryin' me already homez." "He should've known better than that sh*t dawg", he agreed.

When I returned, I was reminded of the "rules of the house" and given an ultimatum regarding whether I wanted to stay there or somewhere else. "I'll go over my aunt's house" I quickly fired. What I really wanted was my father to issue one of his old threats so that he could see who the "real man" of the house was now. The fear that I had of him, as a boy, had long started to dissipate. This wouldn't simply be a beating; it would be murder pure and simple. My mother intervened and said, "We're headed to the mall so get your shoes on."

"What?" I asked. "Ain't goin' to the mall with ya'll." "You ain't stayin' here either" she exclaimed. Man, "Ma" had changed and seemed to favor our abuser more than I ever recalled. I relented and went along to the mall.

I went my separate way in the mall, and ran into the guy that I had stomped out a few days prior. He had two guys with him, one of whom I recognized to be another fellow classmate. He began pointing and I assumed he was sharing the occurrence of the other night with them. I walked on about my business and they followed me through the mall. I turned and approached them, and yelled, "What the f*ck you gone do?" They turned and walked away. As I walked a bit more, believing that the confrontation was over, I saw the group again, and it now numbered five. Shortly thereafter, the cluster had grown into a small mob of eight, and was an assortment of brothers, cousins and my former victim.

"What's up cuz?" one of them asked. "What the f*ck you want it to be dawg?" I responded. "I heard you snuffed my man the other night b*tch, why don't you do that sh*t now nigga?" His face appeared puzzled and then a tad elated when I said, "F*ck it, let's go." I was wearing a pair of Bill Blass overalls and had a pager attached to the bib. I walked hurriedly through the food court, unbuckling my overalls. My little brother begged and pleaded "No, don't!" I drug him as I walked and pushed towards the door leading outside. As soon as the first of the eight emerged behind me, I swung and dropped him. They swarmed me, and I fought with every ounce of strength in my body. I tried to throw one of my assailants over the upper level parking rail to his death. I was absorbing blows but couldn't feel them. I grabbed one in a headlock and his face and my hand travelled through the food court glass which had wire in it, and I lost a piece of my finger.

I continued fighting until the numbers overtook me. I curled up in a ball and protected my head and face. Soon thereafter, I heard security guards running towards the skirmish.

I had a black eye, part of my finger was gone, and had a cut in my eyebrow that required stitches. I got to my feet on my own, and shouted, "It ain't over motherf*ckers!" My parents arrived on the scene, and my mother was crying. I shouted at her, "This is your fault. I told you that I didn't want to come to the mall." I went to the hospital and was pleased to find my attackers there, a few of whom were also seeking medical treatment. The police arrived and wanted to know if I wanted to press charges. "Naw, I'm straight." My father chimed in, "I can have these boys arrested." I thought to myself, "F*ck you man. I don't need you! Never have, never will. I got this." I called Chicago and another of my homies, Reese, and they in turn called some of my other boys. "We on the way baby!" Chicago shouted in his familiar but excited drawl.

Chicago was hurt and I could see his eyes reddening when he reached the hospital. "I should've been there man! I'm gone get these niggas one by one; that's on everything I love dawg." "You know I'm down dawg" I confirmed. I would get pages from on-lookers, concerned females and the like over the next few days. "Nigga, you handled your business. Eight on one! That's some b*tch sh*t, but nigga you represented!" The news spread all over the city like wildfire. My reputation had been revived and expanded. Rivals from old crews even gave me "dap" (a handshake) when they saw me from then on. I was scheduled to report to Marine Combat Training, but never lost contact with Chicago after that. I was still in the state and talked to people back home from time to time as this was a bit different from boot camp; we could make phone calls.

I would find out that Chicago and a few of my other homies were exacting revenge at every turn. They had successfully identified all eight of my assailants and were attacking them both violently and at random, so much to the point that the eight rarely separated due to paranoia. This made me proud. The altercation emboldened me even the more. As I ended Marine Combat Training several weeks later, I had now become extremely proficient at boxing. On the day of graduation, a white Marine called me a n*gger after an exchange of words. As we sat in the locker room assembling our things to be transported out, I fitted my hand with a combination lock, and beat him unconscious leaving large knots all over his face. I only remember the satiating feeling of dominating him physically; everything was black and silent.

Later that day, I learned that my Military Occupational School would be in San Diego, California. I was sickened at the thought of leaving the comfort of my state and even more, having to fly on an airplane that far. I had only seen California on television and the movies, and Washington, D.C. was the furthest north that I'd visited. Nevertheless, I went and credit this experience with marking the beginning of my deconstruction of a centralized mentality. All I ever knew before was my hood, and my city. I had no idea of how vast the country was; I just couldn't conceive of it.

We were stationed on a naval base called Coronado, and the barracks sat right on the beach. In fact, our morning P.T. (physical training) was on the beach each day. I was experiencing culture shock. I rented a car with another Marine, and we rode places after school and on the weekends, and I saw beauty that my eyes had never beheld. As an old song cited, it never rained, and one of the malls didn't even have a roof! I thought I was in heaven. Here, there was no need to worry about being jumped or having to prove myself physically; or at least I thought.

We went to wash the cars one day in hopes of meeting some local girls and instead were "hit up" at gunpoint (approached to find out what gang affiliation we claimed) by some Bloods. "What's poppin' dawg? What set you claim!" Every answer was the wrong answer and I believed that we would die there at that car wash that day. I had committed the unpardonable sin of being caught wearing red in a hood in California. We stood there certain that we would die. With the same spontaneity that they had approached; they sped off. I could hear the gang members laughing and boasting.

We would be given a pass and a brief lesson on territories and boundaries. It was then however that I came to understand the difference between living a gang lifestyle and claiming to be a gang. Real gang members wake up with killing the enemy and surviving the enemy on their minds and are vigilant never to be caught slippin' as we had, because it could mean dying. Nothing comes before the gang; and reppin' colors is a very small and diminishing part of the gang life. I would get a very thorough teaching before my time was done in San Diego.

By the time my departure from California had concluded, I would borrow from the lifestyle important teachings that I would transmit back to my home state in the name of "Bloods". I still managed to cautiously consume the sunshine and mountainous landscapes that California offered. In December, we were given our permanent duty stations, and I was to be stationed only twelve miles from my grandparents' home at Camp LeJeune. I was ecstatic. I could go home every weekend if I wanted. I loved being in California so much though, that I dreaded leaving, and intentionally missed my flight to stay another week. As soon as I arrived in North Carolina at the base, Buddy picked me up from the airport and informed me of the rules and regulations as he recalled them. "You might be in some trouble Buddy" he said. He was right; I received an AWOL (absent without leave) charge as soon as I checked in and was sentenced to duty at the barracks every weekend for a month. The very first weekend that I was allowed to go home coincided with my first paycheck. I was paid my signing bonus, MCT pay and boot camp pay. I had over $13,000 in my pocket. I went to the car lot to buy a car, and because I had no credit, needed someone to sign for me. I asked Buddy, but he couldn't make it to the car lot in time. During the time on fire watch, I had learned that my best friend since 2nd grade was stationed on another part of the base. He was part of our set back home and had left for the Navy two years prior. That weekend, we hooked up, and decided to go back home.

When I couldn't get the car, we looked at each other and laughed because we had more money than we knew what to do with between us. We caught a cab all of the way from Camp LeJeune to Durham, which is more than a two hour drive. The cab driver asked us if we were crazy and we just laughed. When we got home, we got into all kinds of mischief, but one thing was certain, we hadn't missed a beat in the last two years. Just like the old days, we began going home on a regular basis and going up to Chapel Hill chasing girls and fighting locals. We had no fear of reprisal because we were no longer residents; we could always go back to the base hours away. We robbed a lady that one of our friends was selling drugs for, and made off with two handguns and some money from her unlocked car. We stopped going back home for a while until things cooled off. We would go off into the woods and fire the weapon at trees and stand awestricken at how the hallow points destroyed the base of a tree.

We started going to Kinston where my other grandmother resided. I had grown up over the years knowing a beautiful set of twins a few years my junior. My best friend and I would often just keep company with them and nothing romantic ever really developed because they both had boyfriends. It didn't deter us though. "Let's go see the twins", my best friend urged. "Alright" I said, and we were on the road to drive the forty miles that we drove maybe two to three times a week. Often when we made the journey we would dare each other to do outlandish things. Neither of us would ever let the other down when it came to taking the dare. "I bet you won't pull over and shoot the gun out of the window" I challenged. "What? Boy you know better than that; pull over!" he responded with confidence. "Boom!!!!" and we sat half deaf laughing at our willingness to do anything imaginable.

As we travelled to see the twins that night, a deer standing alongside the road would meet his end because of a dare. "Boom!!!!" "Oh sh*t, did you see the skin peel back?" Nothing repulsed us, and more than anything, both of us were young, crazy and willing to kill to demonstrate our loyalty to the other. This would prove almost immediately, to be a recipe for disaster. *We were "soldiers."*

CHAPTER 10: DOIN' TIME

It was freezing, and I stood there with my eyes closed tight, and swallowed like I had so many times before when I anticipated pain. The last vision that I had was of the barrel pointing towards my face. I heard the hammer fall and I saw the previous eighteen years flash across my face. "You better kill me nigga!!!" I screamed. We stood no more than five feet apart. There had been words exchanged through a woman, one he was dating, and thought that I wanted. Here, in this moment, it had come to a head, and I stood defenseless, with nothing to protect my person except for my fear of nothing. I had prepared my mind for this type of death; I simply thought I would be granted more time. I didn't flinch; I simply felt my chest to see if I was hit. I wasn't, and I heard the hammer fall again and seemingly jam. My best friend leapt into action grabbing a .12 gauge shotgun from behind the passenger's seat and handing me a .9mm. By this time, my would-be murderers had jumped into their vehicle and tried to flee. It was too late; we opened fire. I saw the side of the car turn white from the shells in the shotgun. Glass shattered and I saw one head disappear from view. "We got that muthaf*cka!!!" my friend yelled. The car trailed out of sight and we gave chase in my car. I banged my fists against the steering wheel. I turned to my friend and vowed, "We gotta finish this!" The car would later meet with a telephone pole.

We returned to the city the next two days later and went onto the grounds of the local high school. The campus was abuzz about the shooting. "I walked with my pistol in my jacket asking guys, "Where the f*ck is Calvin?" "He ain't been to school in a couple of days", one kid said. "What's his boy's name?" I inquired. "I heard he was in the hospital", someone retorted. "He ain't dead!" I asked. "I don't know" he cautiously responded. My intention was to egregiously murder them both right there in the school. I had no regard for the repercussions and we hunted them tirelessly for the next few days.

I had been violated. Someone had dared pull a gun on me and didn't kill me. I had always heard the old heads in the hood say, "man if a nigga pull a gun on me, he better kill me!" This statement guided the pattern of my responses. I reckoned that any person willing to try and kill me once would surely do so again. I had survived being shot at from close range. This only added to my belief that I could not die. We rode around and looked for his house. "I'm gone kill this nigga's mama if he ain't home. It's that b*tch's fault for havin' his ass!" At this point, I didn't recognize myself; I had snapped. My perception of reality had been distorted beyond the bounds of human compassion.

Before there could be another confrontation, I was asked to report back to the barracks, which I thought to be strange. I had planned to travel back to my hometown that evening, along with my best friend to round up some of our former set. When I reached the barracks, all of the brass was there, as well as the unit's Gunnery Sergeant. "What's going on?" I asked. "These gentlemen need to speak with you Lewis" he replied. These "gentlemen" turned out to be the N.I.S. I thought they were here to confront me about the shooting. I began explaining how I was simply defending myself, but they were investigating threats made against two other Marines. Evidently, I had come into the barracks in the middle of the night and pointed my gun at my roommates and robbed them of their personal belongings. In actuality, I had come in and told them briefly about the incident I was involved in days before and allowed my roommate to clean the pistol for me, after which I left. I never resided in the barracks. My account of what happened did not matter. I was placed into custody, and my vehicle was searched. The guns from the shooting were recovered, and a nightmare ensued.

The date was February 12th, 1992. I was stripped of all of my belongings; my dress blues, my cammies (camouflage uniform), everything. I swore to myself "when I get out, I am going to track down those two white boys and kill both of them for lying." I thought, as soon as I get to court, there's no way I would be convicted of something I didn't do. Little did I know that revenge would be the least of my concerns over the next few months. I was brought in late that evening, probably about 9 p.m. and processed. I was treated respectfully compared to the times I would be incarcerated in the future. First the man behind the desk asked for my shoestrings, then my belt, then all of my clothes. I thought that I was being stripped searched. I had heard about this happening to prisoners before, and here I was cold and naked in front of another man. I was handcuffed again, and placed in the first cell on the block. "You understand that this is for your safety?" he asked. "We're putting you on suicide watch for at least forty-eight hours" he offered. There I sat on a two-inch gym mat for two days, bare-bottomed, shivering and afraid. Other prisoners walked by and leered at me; some told me to stay strong, while others just looked at me as if I were a lunatic. I had heard never to show fear in prison or it could lead to you being raped. So I glared at everyone that walked by with a look of bold defiance.

There was a small chrome toilet in the corner. The bars were beige and the paint was peeling. An elderly white gentleman's face appeared at the bars after about three days, and asked if I was okay. He wasn't wearing military fatigues, and looked to be fairly trustworthy. "I'm okay. I just want my clothes." "We'll see what we can do about that", he uttered. I assumed at that time that he was a chaplain or some human rights' advocate. Soon I was asked to walk backwards to the cell door and place my hands through the bars. I was handcuffed and then shackled. I was slowly walked to a cell with a bed and given a t-shirt, underwear and prison-issued pants!

I quickly came into the knowledge that I was in a maximum security cell, and anytime I moved throughout the prison, I would be handcuffed to my own waist, shackled and the entire facility would be notified and locked down. I didn't quite understand why I had been placed here. As talk circulated my row, I found that I was placed amidst inmates considered to be the most dangerous. One inmate, "Stan", had allegedly committed double-murder and I would find out later that another had several counts of child molestation. Further down the row, one guy had been charged with murdering his infant child, and another an alleged arsonist that had killed several Marines in his unit. I was now eighteen and sat amongst alleged murderers, rapists and child molesters.

For a long period of time, I would languish in curiosity as to why I was here. I went to trial eventually, and as though it were but a simple procedure, I was not allowed to testify, face my accusers, and was subsequently found guilty of all charges. I was sentenced to a year, but had my time reduced to six months. I could then begin the business of counting down. During the next couple of months, I was transitioned to general population where there were rooms littered with bodies behind a huge fence. I was afraid to go to sleep, because I had been shown who the rapists were already.

The sudden movements, the screams, the moans from men masturbating and the fights were pounding on my psyche, but I could never show weakness; not for an instant. There was a guy that was about 320 lbs, standing about 6'3 that had been charged and convicted of roughly sixty counts of sodomy. Story had it that he would pick up Marines walking back to base, render them unconscious by punching them, and hence they would awaken to being sodomized. I told myself that even at 175 lbs soaking wet, I would not be a victim, and I kept my eyes on him during meals and out in the yard. I quickly aligned myself with anyone claiming "Blood" regardless of their set. My paranoia was later quelled by the fact that I was moved back to maximum security. I was treated as though I had murdered someone. Then it occurred to me that perhaps the guy that we shot at must have died over the last few days. I became distraught, and thought that I would never get out of prison again.

I was ashamed to let anyone know where I was. I was told the mail would be opened and read, and any objectionable material would be destroyed or marked out. Letters mailed out of the facility would undoubtedly inform people of where I was, so I opted to keep my incarceration a secret. The nights were long, and I was tortured by the sounds of the inmates masturbating and threatening each other. No one on my row was eligible for outside or recreational time, save the aforementioned lockdown. We all did pushups and sit-ups using the bars for exercise. Showers were taken in front of the guards in handcuffs and were timed. Showers and legal visits were the only time we journeyed from our cells. There was no television and my food was served under the bars of the cell. There was a wall right in front of my cell, so days and nights ran together. We would ask the guards what time it was as an exercise of staying connected.

It would take a while before I became "acclimated" to my surroundings. I felt somewhat like I did as a child, having to sit idly by and powerless as the screams of someone's violation invaded my cell. There were no headphones to put on, and the pillows were failures at muffling the rapes. The victim was typically the same one; a man named "Beeks", who had been accused of several charges of child molestation. To my knowledge, he had largely gone unfettered until his trial approached and was written about in the local paper.

Beeks was a white man in his forties who wore very distinguished gold-framed glasses. He was relatively soft-bodied and appeared to pose no threat to anyone. In addition, he was always talking on the row about his love for Jesus. He would quote scripture upon scripture, and always offer that he would pray for me and others as he was released on Sundays for church service. His ramblings were many times muted by threats from Zulu who resided on the other side of him furthest from my cell. Zulu was a Muslim who had been incarcerated for conscientious objection to the conflict in Saudi Arabia.

Zulu, was a small African American man standing only about 5'3 at best, but commanded his end of the cell block presumably by the way he ordered the guards around and was largely boisterous during quiet time. He had a very large nose and wore a boxed haircut with his prison issued uniform sagging fashionably. I was impressed with Zulu's defiance but steered clear of engaging him verbally for a few months. Much of his discernable dialogue had to do with firearms and "whipping Beeks' ass" if he said another word. Beeks would simply begin crying as if he knew that Zulu would make good on his threats.

As I sat pondering my inescapable surroundings and eating my dinner, a handful of the others would customarily be released from their cells to eat at a table situated between the ends of the rows. I would sit very still and chew softly so that I might hear a whisper of television. Much to my chagrin, the voices typically carried overwhelmingly and made the television shows that I longed to simply hear, inaudible. My hope of experiencing a small piece of the routine on the outside would be repeatedly pilfered. I wondered what people were doing, whether or not they were thinking of me, or if any one missed my presence. "How was the world still functioning without me out there?" I yelled inside my head for months. The retort was simple; it just does.

Perhaps even louder than the pounding of rhetorical questions bouncing against the sides of my mind were the screams of Beeks at dinner. For as hard as I tried to press my young face against the bars of my cell and look down the row, I could never see, only imagine what was happening. I listened to how he begged and pleaded. Why were they doing this? The newspaper finally made it to my cell days later, and I read of Beeks' charges. My voice pierced the air one afternoon, and

I asked of Beeks, "Did you do it man? Did you have sex with those kids?" My street-rearing dictated that I be repulsed at his very sight; that he deserved every bad thing imaginable for killing innocence. As usual, Beeks began crying, and cited that 'he had sinned and asked God for forgiveness'. "So you did do it!" I yelled. Though our (my brother and I) abuse was never sexual, I held a murderous disdain in my bowel for anyone that had subjected a child to anything close to what we experienced.

At first the guards would stand by my cell and talk to me to distract me from what was happening around the corner. Armed with Beeks' confession, I expeditiously failed to care anymore, and at once, I no longer heard his cries and ignored his conversation down the row. He was dying his death, and I was dying mine. I was secluded and being victimized by my own thoughts. I recall looking for someone to blame, and then it occurred to me that my reckless abandon had led me to this place that I knew was inevitable. I could only blame myself, and with that, I became suicidal yet again. I was granted help that was inexplicably timely.

That familiar elderly white face re-appeared at the bars one day and genuinely asked of me, "How are you son? How are they treating you?" His voice was a calming force amidst all of the clamoring iniquity that surrounded me on a minute to minute basis. He would appear from time to time and ask me about my feelings, my childhood and symptoms of my behaviors. I began looking forward to the prison psychologist stopping by. Many times, I would ask questions simply to have some conversation to pass the time; I was lonely.

The next person to actively engage me was "Godfather". He was a tall thin man with dark-skin and very long straightened salt and pepper hair. He was cool, and pimped as such when he walked. He had the respect of everyone on the row. Even the guards respected Godfather. When he spoke, we all listened. Evidently, he had also earned the privilege of driving the book cart down the cell block and he would drop a book off as he passed every now and then. It was while I was on suicide watch and lie naked on a vinyl mattress that he offered me a dictionary and a couple of literary novels. He was working on several degree programs from "inside" and was in all senses of the word, what we called a "jail-house lawyer."

I finally decided to write my then high school sweetheart, though I was dishonest about my whereabouts. She wrote back and sent provocative pictures. By this time, I had learned the system of passing material through the bars atop the cell. I showed her picture to Godfather. He said to me, "man this girl is beautiful, but ask yourself, if you're in here, who took these pictures?" I was crushed, and that was the last time that I wrote her. The outside world was on a different schedule, had different concerns, and I had to understand, that I was no longer one of them.

Godfather urged me to read and would often quiz me from his end of the row and ask my interpretation of texts. He nicknamed me, "Machinegun." I asked what the name meant. He said because I was originally processed with weapons charges, there was a gun called a Lewis machinegun, and that HE felt that such a moniker was appropriate. The first title that he shared was Dr. Francis Cress Welsing's, *The Isis Papers: The Keys to the Colors.* I felt such tremendous pressure to return the text that I poured over its pages and tried to hurriedly return it to him. When he passed by one day, I offered it to him, and he said quite sternly, "read it again." I didn't argue, but I realized on the second read that the level of abstraction that lay within these pages would take literally years for me to consume and reckon.

Throughout the next weeks, Godfather showed me how to order books from outside of the prison and have them shipped to me. I read the FBI files on Malcolm X and was slowly introduced to another kind of militancy. I was both astonished and ashamed of who I was, and the fact that I had ever joined the military to start with. Once it became evident to me that Hoover had gone to such great lengths to retard the freedom of my people, I felt as though everything I ever learned about this country was a falsehood. I felt betrayed two-fold. I had vowed to defend democracy with my life, and now I sat within prison walls for a crime I didn't commit and learning more than I ever did in school. My favorite text during my incarceration would become a book by a man named Webster.

I began to read the Holy Bible and the Holy Qu'Ran interchangeably and engage Zulu in debates about apparent contradictions that I discovered. I was being exposed to a truth that I had never heard in church. I then studied Confucianism and Buddhism. I became a sponge and the days and nights began to become as one. In retrospect, books served as a vehicle. Literature allowed me to transcend the walls of the brig, and escape to faraway places, ride beautiful horizons that I could not physically see and live during times that were an impossibility. In books, I could be anyone and anything that my heart secretly desired and most of all, I was free. For the first time since my childhood, I dreamed again. Still, the reality of my environment beat down upon my conscience like torrential rains on dry earth.

I grew so lonesome and truly suicidal that I finally took the opportunity to make a call one weekend. I called my grandfather, whose gun I had stolen to exact revenge on Calvin. My grandmother answered the phone, and I told her that I was in Norway with my unit, and I needed to speak with my grandfather. "Buddy, I'm in the brig. Please don't tell Mama", I begged. He had worked and retired on the base that I was incarcerated on, so he knew how to get to where I was. "I won't tell her son, it would kill her." On Saturdays, I would look up, and a guard would say, "You have a visitor". As soon as I was shackled and handcuffed, the loud speaker throughout the prison would announce: "Lockdown that is lockdown, cease all prisoner movement until further notice!" I never got used to that announcement. In essence, it meant that I was a murderer.

The first visit was heart-wrenching for both of us. "I told your mama that I went to the store. I hate lying to her, but I know she would worry herself to death." His eyes turned a pinkish tint, and a tear flowed from both evenly. "Why son? Why did you take the gun and get involved in this mess? I feel like this is all my fault; if I had locked it up..." he started. "Buddy, I had my mind made up and I would've done what I was planning anyway. Don't blame yourself. "This ain't how we raised you" he offered as another set of tears erupted from his eyes and found themselves trapped between the wrinkles. "Daddy, I love you, I'm okay. Now please go home before mama suspects something." "I'll see you next weekend Buddy" he said and I watched him gather his aging frame and reluctantly trudge towards the door, as if anchored by some invisible weight.

When I returned to my cell, I wept as a child uncontrollably. I had hurt and disappointed the man who had taught me how to love and be respectful of others. Most of all, I had involved him, and he too was a casualty of my rage. He didn't deserve this; the wheels were spinning out of control, and now I had only regret.

Months would pass before anyone else would come to know of my whereabouts. My grandfather had even lied to my mother when asked where I was. On a subsequent visit, he admonished me to contact her, because her concern was more than he could bear. I decided that he had done enough, and it wasn't fair to ask him to deceive the people he loved. I contacted my mother on a collect call, and told her where I was. I asked her not to mention it to my father; she refused. A couple of weeks passed and instead of seeing my grandfather in the visiting room, it was my mother accompanied by her brother and "Him". My mother burst into tears, and screamed, "Why is he chained up like an animal, that's my baby?!!!!" My father comforted her, and our eyes failed to meet. After all, I think we both could concede that there was a history between he and I that partly led me here. In a professional demeanor that he always maintained with me, he asked how they were treating me, to which I responded, "I'm alright." The visit proved to be too much for my mother, and was abbreviated. I had said that if I ever got out of this place, I would never return.

The State Bureau of Investigations sent two detectives to talk to me about the murder that occurred just prior to my incarceration. My name was given as the assailant in the crime. I spoke freely with investigators without counsel, and found myself scheduled for a polygraph the following week. "You can tell us if you killed the guy, he was scum, he was a drug dealer and hell, to be honest with you, if I could've killed him and got away with it, I would have. We can help you, if you just tell us how everything transpired." I was out of my cell, eating meals and drinking sodas with my hands free. While it may sound sick and depraved at this point, I was actually enjoying myself. I had food; real food, and someone to talk to.

I actually looked forward to the detectives coming to take me to their office. I painted myself into a corner, because I proceeded to tell the detectives the story that I had told the authorities upon my arrest, failing miserably to realize that the victim of the homicide was a different individual.

During the polygraph, I was asked if I had ever been involved in a shooting incident, to which I answered yes. I was asked if I had killed a gentleman the detectives called by name to which I responded no. I was asked if I ever wanted to kill someone, to which I answered yes, and a litany of other questions that had little to do with the incident. The results of the polygraph were "inconclusive." The detectives didn't come around for a few weeks. When they did return, they had a signed statement from my best friend, whom I found out was now incarcerated in the same prison. I read his statement that said I had done all of the shooting and he had tried to dissuade me. I got a "runner" (someone with free movement in prison by virtue of job assignment) to pass notes to him, and he replied that he had made the statement because the detectives told him that I had written a similar statement saying that he was the shooter. I felt betrayed and believed my fate to be sealed. This was a guy I had known since second grade, we had banged the same set, and he had tried to put the needle in my arm!

I was held in the prison for months until the ballistics tests proved that the weapons that were in my possession at the time of my arrest were not the murder weapons. The charges were dropped, and I again focused on what I would do upon being released. So many days and nights passed without my ever seeing the sunshine. I will never forget the brightness of the sun as I walked with back to the brig. It was as though God had used it to force tears from this hardened soul, and simply whispered "today I have righted your path and blessed the rest of your days." Such plans proved to be a bit premature and in vain. I walked outside of the prison, and was taken to an office and given instructions not to return to the base and that my discharge status would be characterized as a BCD (Bad Conduct Discharge). As I prepared to leave and start my life anew, authorities from the county of where the murder charge originated placed me under arrest. I was charged with discharging a firearm within the city limits, which was a felony.

The processing in county jail was different, and unfortunately a process that I would undergo many more times. "Drop your drawers. Bend over and touch your toes. Spread your butt cheeks. Open your mouth, tilt your head back and lift your tongue" were the orders barked by corrections officers. "What?" This was the most demeaning and dehumanizing part of being locked up. I never got used to having another man peering into my rectum with gloves on for a weapon. As soon as I received my prison issued uniform, I was escorted to my cell.

My bunkmate introduced himself, and told me which bunk was his. I awoke the next morning to the shuffle of shower shoes, and men huddled by the bars; it was about 5:30 a.m. "Breakfast!" the guard yelled. I gathered my bowl of grits and walked back to my cell. As soon as I entered, my bunkmate said, "What's up wit' dem grits?", and punched me in my face. My grits spilled and we fought bitterly for a moment, until I gained the advantage and slammed his head against the toilet several times. As quickly as it began, it was over, and we both breathed heavily as he moaned in agony. This was a discussion that we would not need to have again. This served notice to all of the other inmates that I was not easy pickings, nor was my food available for the taking. After about two months, my father arranged bail and the charges would later be dismissed. "I went to school with the district attorney down here boy, and she did me a favor" he explained. I still didn't care. I was relieved to be out, but this would be momentarily also.

I returned to Durham and took to running the streets, living from place to place, inclusive of my car, friend's floors, abandoned houses and new constructions. No one wanted much to do with me except for Chicago. My habit of breaking into new constructions for a night of sleep would not be prevalent as I was awakened by a man pointing a gun at me one morning. He just asked that I move along. My life had once again been spared. My aunt felt sorry for me, and allowed me to live with her and her two children for a while. I found refuge with a friend named "Reese", who allowed me to sleep in his room after his mother had fallen asleep most nights. Reese stood about 6'5 and was about 185. Reese was nice with his hands, and seldom had problems with anyone. He had long arms and a very dark bumpy face, with bright pink lips. He had gone to barber school while I had gone to the military.

We were all hanging out in a hood called the "West End" one day, riding around in my car. As the police moved in behind us, Reese began to cuss. Unbeknownst to me, he had stashed a bag of crack cocaine under the seat in the car, right beside my gun that I had let him borrow a few days prior. "Get out of the car with your hands above your head!" blared over the megaphone. "Just do what he says and we good", I told Reese and Chicago. Nothing could have been farther from the truth. The police man cited that there was a random drug check going on in the area, so he would need to search the vehicle. Reese said, "It ain't my car, you gotta ask him", pointing to me. I consented, and when the police brought the gun, crack and scale to me to identify, Reese wouldn't look at me. "Tell me whose this is, and we can clear this up" urged the officer. Nobody said anything, so they split us up. I had given up selling crack long ago, but I knew the gun was mine, and fingerprints would reveal this fact, so I claimed the gun. Reese and Chicago said nothing still, and so we were all charged with the drugs and the paraphernalia. I thought being a standup guy made me a man, but it just made me stupid. I caught a break downtown because of my military I.D. and eventually plead to carrying a concealed weapon. Reese and I hung out less after that.

Chicago and I returned to our previous employment of breaking and entering, stealing VCRs, DVD players, and camcorders. I began running with guys from school, and scouting houses that we planned to hit. If one of my boys called and said, "I got a lick", that meant that he had scoped out a home, and was now knowledgeable of what time the inhabitants would come and go. This cycle of stealing and pawning ran its course, and came to a conclusion when there was a miscalculation in one of the licks. I popped the window, a craft I learned how to facilitate quietly, and we entered the residence like we always did. He began casing the house, and I began stuffing our bag. I felt a tad uneasy because I had warned Chicago about daytime licks, but I didn't care; I needed the cash. All of a sudden he came running, and fell down the stairs trying to maintain his balance, and yelled, "Someone's in here…he's got a gun!!!!!" We bolted the same way we came in and ran through the woods hiding. We ran through the woods and tried to make out way back to our vehicle parked a few houses away. We heard sirens, and my heart raced. I couldn't go back to jail. I was exhausted from running in the heat, and almost suddenly, I passed out in the grass, and fell asleep.

When I came to, it was dusk and I walked casually to my car with no clue of what happened to Chicago. A few days later, I was arrested for possession of stolen goods as the pawn shop had kept accurate records of all the items we were pawning. Chicago and I would be charged with over sixty-five counts of breaking and entering, ranging from homes to vehicles. I was sick on my stomach. All I could do was envision the cell door closing and prepare to ward off predators again. Prison was a game of survival and I was fast becoming a regular player. While awaiting my court date on this charge, I would find myself amidst another shooting incident. I was riding with a co-worker named Terrance and we were on our way to pick up a girl that I had gotten pregnant from a nearby city where she was working. As we passed through the town, we were unsure of where to turn, and a car flicked the lights on and off behind us, blowing the horn and driving erratically. Terrance said, "Pull over to the side." He retrieved a revolver from his coat as we got behind the car. He leaned out of the window and started shooting. It was actually funny until cops blocked the car in and drew guns on us, outside of the girl's workplace. "Freeze or we'll shoot!!!!!" All I could think was that I might get shot this time. These cops were white, we were in the middle of nowhere, and they seemed angry. They even made her get on the ground, pregnant and all. There with headlights shining in my face, I was on my knees, with my hands interlocked over my head, wondering how I got here; so far away from innocence, so far away from normalcy.

My bond was revoked, and I would not soon be released on these charges, and before it was all said and done, I would see my parents put up their house to get me out because my bond was so high. Months passed this time, and there were no letters, no visits and few phone calls. I now had a child on the way, and there I sat in jail. Terrance was out before the weekend was over, and he left me there. What did I expect? Someone so callous was incapable of doing the right thing. I had made up in my mind that when I walked in to this jail, I would make my mark early.

There was a guy in the cell block from Durham, and he had all of the other inmates frightened. He yelled at the guards, and the very next morning after I arrived, took a guy's breakfast. From what I understood, he took it every morning. The guy just sat on his bunk and cried. I said, "Why don't you leave him alone man; at least let him eat!" "F*ck you, I'll take your food nigga!!!" he responded. We faced off, and the guards intervened by banging their nightsticks against the bars. I couldn't rest, and as I attempted to sleep I revisited my childhood habit of gritting my teeth and chewing the inner portion of my jaw. In my mind, it was far from over. He had both threatened me, as well as presented me with an opportunity to seize respect and control of the cell.

The next morning, the same script played out, with this guy "punking" the smaller, and taking his breakfast. The television was scheduled to play one channel, and this guy took a stick made of newspaper with a pencil in the end and turned the channel. When the guards turned it back, he waited a while and took the "remote" and knocked it from the stand smashing it. There was an uproar in the cell, and we were informed that there would be no replacement. Shortly thereafter we were scheduled to clean the cell. We were given ammonia to mop the cell floor, of which I retained a little in a coffee cup. When one of the guys asked for a "light" later in the day to warm his coffee over the makeshift heater he made over the toilet, I snagged a match. That night at lights out, I waited and waited until I heard the cell bully snoring. I poured the ammonia around the corners of his mattress and lit the match. He awoke screaming and begged to be moved to another cell. He was placed in protective custody, and I never had to rouse from sleep another morning, because my breakfast and a little extra was always under my bunk.

When I was released this time, I was determined to turn things around, I had made up my mind to move enough drugs to subsidize a lawyer and beat the charges; this proved to be another failed attempt at leaving the streets. I returned again to sleeping wherever I could, and finally got an apartment and a "front" job. I hooked up with Reese again, who had agreed to help me make money, because he had a child on the way as well. Just as we did in high school, Reese and I hopped into my car and decided to go to the "Hill" as we called it. Reese had to drive because my license was suspended at the time. As we prepared to leave Reese's house, we pulled up to a traffic light and we saw Chicago, who had been in all sorts of trouble lately. We had also found out that the police were actively looking for him for the murder back in Illinois, so everybody was avoiding him at the time. "Where ya'll headed?" he asked with his characteristic thick-tongued speech. "To the Hill" I said, as Reese interrupted loudly saying "Nowhere!" "Let me roll man!" Chicago begged. "Hell naw" Reese exclaimed. "Come on ya'll" Chicago pleaded again. "Get in the back" I relented.

Reese leaned forward and looked at me as if I were just simply stupid. The look would serve as a premonition that haunts me to this day. Chicago piled into the back with a huge black coat on, and yelled out of the window all the way to Chapel Hill. Intermittently Reese would look at me and shake his head. "Don't be doing no stupid shit when we get up here man", Reese said with an over the shoulder glance at Chicago. At that moment Chicago pulled a Tech .22 from his jacket and shouted, "look what I copped ya'll." We almost ran off the road, as Reese and I ducked. "Put that sh*t away fool!!!!" Reese screamed. "Ain't nothing gone…." Chicago attempted to retort. At that very instant the gun went off about eight or nine times out of the window. "What the hell is wrong with you?!!" I hollered at Chicago. "My fault, my man said it had a hair trigger" Chicago said with a blank look on his face. "I told yo' ass" Reese said to me, with an overtone of chastening. Reese pulled the car over to the side of the road and we all took turns yelling at each other.

After a while we resumed our trip after agreeing that Reese and Chicago would not hang together once we got to the "Hill." Once we arrived, Reese dropped us off and went to look for a parking space. Chicago jumped out the car walking ahead of me. A white couple was fast approaching as we walked up towards the strip. Before I knew it Chicago grabbed the guy by his shirt and pulled out the gun. "Gimme your wallet….and take off all yo' clothes!!!!" I was frozen; I literally couldn't move. The first thought that crossed my mind was that these poor souls were about to die if they resisted Chicago. He had the gun in the guy's mouth and flashes of the hair trigger going off almost made me urinate on myself. Chicago walked the couple to the strip naked, and I turned and ran; but it was too late. I would find out later that there was a small police station at the intersection where Chicago had spared their lives. I ran towards Reese in the car, running and out of breath. "Chicago is trippin', let's go!" I panted. I heard sirens, and before I could reach the car to get in, the police were coming down the street. "Run!!! I'll find you later" Reese shouted.

I ran down several streets, dashed between a few student housing buildings and finally laid down behind some bushes for a while. After catching my breath, my mind returned to Reese's last words to me, "I'll find you later." I knew he wouldn't leave me with my own car. All I wanted was to find him, and get out of Chapel Hill. I ended up about three miles from the strip and emerged from the bushes by a store, where I saw Reese riding around slowly. I dashed across the street and tried to get his attention, and as soon as I made my way into the parking lot of the store on foot, there I was, trapped by two police cars. "Freeze!!!" they shouted. I knew the drill, so without prompting I put my hands in the air and stood as still as I could, swallowing dry spittle. A cop across the street had Chicago up against the car. I was asked for my I.D. and we were walked to the same car. Suddenly, Chicago snatched away from the officer that was trying to cuff him, and climbed a fence by a car wash. "Freeze or I'll shoot!!!!" the officer warned. I have no clue what spoke to me at that moment, but I broke loose in the other direction, running towards the tree line. "Freeze or I'll shoot" he repeated and I heard the leather holster release from the hand of my potential executioner. Branches hit me in my mouth and eyes and I could not see anything in front of me. A small part of me had prayed that this officer wouldn't shoot me in my back, but I also knew that I couldn't answer to these charges alone.

Over the course of the night, I ran from police dogs stopping to rest from time to time, until their barks would get louder. I knew the dogs would gather my scent and this footrace would end soon. I had briars in my cheek and it almost seemed worthless to keep running. In an instant I took about a ten foot drop and landed in a small body of water. My leg was injured and I couldn't get up. I heard the dogs again and I heard an officer say, "I think we got him!" I saw the breaking of light in the bushes overhead, so I held my breath and submerged my head beneath the water. I stayed there for what felt like forever, fighting to stay conscious. My head floated to the top and I had decided to give up, so I stood up with my hands in the air, but to my amazement, the dogs and police had moved on. The barking became faint and it was dark again. I sat back down in the water and gathered myself. I waited for almost an hour before deciding to move on. I worked desperately to get out of the hole I'd fallen into. I walked gingerly through the woods until I came to an empty house. I entered and collapsed into a deep slumber. I was awakened by a white man that startled me. "Don't shoot me!" I screamed. "I'm not going to shoot you. Are you okay, you're bleeding?" he shared. "I'm sorry", I said sliding on my butt away from him, "I'll leave." "Do you need a ride to the hospital?" he asked. "No, can you take me to Durham?" I asked. "Sure" he replied.

I crawled into his van, and got a ride to my aunt's house. I shared my story with her and asked if I could lay low for a couple of days. I heard from Chicago about two days later. He described the same ordeal, but said he got back to Durham by stealing a moped. He had put himself up in a room with the fruits of his robbery. I decided to wait a couple of days and then go by Reese's house. When I did, he met me at the door with my clothes and my car keys. "You gotta go" he said. "You can't stay over here anymore." He explained. I was crushed, because Reese had put me up most nights. He stayed with his mom, so I was able to pilfer a good meal when he ate in his room. "Have the cops been by?" I asked of him. "Yeah, but they were looking for Chicago" he responded. We rehashed what happened and I left feeling like this was the end of our friendship. I called my mother who I hadn't spoken to in over a year, and asked if I could come back home. She said that I could return for a couple of nights; the offer would be made in vain.

My son was born that night, for which I was in attendance. I fell asleep on the floor in my old room until the doorbell rung early that next morning. I was supposed to go back to the hospital but the authorities had requested my presence downtown. My father told them he would surrender me to save the embarrassment of me being cuffed and placed in the car. The officer consented and I prepared myself once again to go back inside. I was not given a bond so I stayed behind bars for a long time this time. I was even more miserable this time. When the bars closed this time, something inside me said that it would be forever. The guys in my cell started prophetically calling me "Teacher" because my language skills were a little more polished because of my reading in prison. I would be asked to write letters, read letters and help with phrasing requests for attorneys. I requested one major piece of mail to be sent; the most important I would ever receive. Months ago, I had applied to college from prison. I was accepted, but I still had to make it out of court.

On January 4th, 1994, my mother accompanied me to court, where I had planned to plead guilty to common law robbery as a condition for having all of my other charges dismissed. My public defender could not tell me whether my plea would garner active time, but did advise me to "take the deal". The district attorney was an African American man who was notorious for punishing black defendants with harsh sentences. He wouldn't even look at me while he told the judge that I had robbed a collegiate couple with an assault weapon. My lawyer said that because I was there when Chicago robbed the couple,

I was guilty of a lesser felony. The judge asked me what my part in the robbery was and I told him. Something that day emboldened me to look the judge directly in his eye and tell the truth. He resounded that since I did not report the crime, that I was as guilty of robbing the exchange students as if I had the gun.

When I returned from the stand to sit beside my lawyer, I walked past Chicago. He leaned forward in his seat, and simply said, "I'm gonna take all of the charges." As our lawyers conferenced he said, "man you got a son, and you trying to go to school. They got me on all kinds of sh*t. I got it." At that very moment, the lawyers walked over to the judge and then stepped back. The judge then ordered me to stand. He said, "I see you are a veteran and have been accepted to college. I can tell that you have some potential and obviously want to turn things around, however these are very serious charges. I hereby order you to serve a period of no longer than seven years in a state penal institution." A lump rose in my throat and I felt the tears welling in my eyes, and just as they were about to spill over, I looked at my public defender, who eyes were pointed at the floor, and I heard the judge trail off, "to be suspended for a period of five years. You have an opportunity to turn your life around. This is my personal promise to you young man; go to school and stay out of the city of Durham, because if I see you again in this courtroom you will do the entire seven years that I have suspended today and the full sentence for any new charges!" I sat in that courtroom for a few minutes afraid to move. Was I free to go, or would there be more charges awaiting me on the other side of the door? I was intensely afraid, but one thing was for certain, this had to be my last trip inside of a courtroom as a defendant.

Unlike many of the hardened men that I heard characterize their apathy about the prospects of returning to prison, I did not share their enthusiasm. Prison had changed me, parts of me for the better, and some for the worst. I had lost a measure of autonomy forever, and I would forever be frozen in moments that bystanders couldn't fathom. I developed triggers for defense mechanisms that have sabotaged my ability to trust others. Gray areas faded away, and I became absolute in my dealings with people; things were either one way or the other, there could exist no "in between". Prison would, for a long time to come, rob me of my ability to know love holistically, because I assessed threats and the presence of ulterior motives as a primary function and believed that caring might lead to my own casualty.

Prison is a predicament peculiar to those who have experienced its vices. It seemingly seizes certain character traits that were innate and uncalculated, and changes them forever; turning them into a process. What had I left on the inside? I had wrestled precious tears from the eyes of Buddy. I had caused Mama's intuition to lead her to prayer on my behalf because she "knew somethin' just wasn't right." I had actuated the label once affixed to me in the street. My life had been marred by so many things that spiraled out of control so radically that I had no other alternative but to learn now to fight in a different manner, or perish by the violence that had all but engulfed me since my presence on earth.

I would begin with the single mission of proving everyone wrong. I had ample opportunity during my incarceration to replay all of the negative characterizations about me. I had long ceased seeking the approval of my parents, as I was certain that they both hated me. I would recall the face of my fourth grade teacher; every beating, and each tussle with "Man", the nights in the car with Chicago, whom had essentially just handed me my life back; the betrayal by my former friend and more so than anything, the sheer anguish in the face of the only man that embraced and believed in me. I would amass them all together and heap them upon my shoulders, which the world had made so broad, and my successes would become punitive to those who had written me off.

I was fueled by a new fury. I wanted more than anything, my father's respect as a man; being his son was never an option. I wanted my mother to experience flying vicariously through my existence. I wanted my brother to see that we were not defined by our upbringing and that my wings, though tattered, could heal. Prison was not the end for me; it was in fact my personal renaissance. It had equipped me with my life's passion and the blueprint for my destiny. Doin' time meant that my wings were only broken for a season.

CHAPTER 11: STILL BROKEN

"What's wrong with you?" This would become a question that fell from the lips of most every woman I've ever been with. Some of the most beautiful women that God has created have tried their hand at loving me, or "fixing" me, all to walk away taking some of my pain along with them. I wish that I could say, I've never treated a woman the way my father did my mother; that I had never raised my hand in anger, or that the mental cruelty had never been inflicted on those caring souls, but that would be a lie. Some have been more patient than others, and some have come to extract from me what they could, but the truth of the matter is, none of them, not one, has had all of my heart.

The greater majority of them, reminded me of my mother in some way. Perhaps they were timid or shared her long hair and natural beauty. I made it a rule never to date a woman that needed make-up. It has always been much easier for me to give than to receive, because receiving in my mind always required relinquishing part of myself. Further, I had determined that I would never trust a soul. In even more recent years, I have come to understand where this feeling of distrust was born. In the face of lovely women crying and pleading with me to give them one more chance and professing their love for me, my heart waxed cold and I chuckled inside. "Look at her" I thought. "Am I supposed to believe that you love me, when my own parents don't?"

Along the way, I lost the ability to feel as deeply; I'm impervious to certain pains at the hands of others; refusing to be a victim again, keep the world at arm's length always doubting the motive of those who profess to love or care. In this manner, domestic violence has wrestled from me a victory that I am to numb to truly realize lost; my highs are not as high yet my lows are even lower. I pray for the day when I can look forward in not only spirit but in truth, not looking behind or contrasting my hopes against the realities of those horrible things that happened. I know that there is so much more to passing this way, within this seeming hamster wheel of life. It is only through my suffering that the smallest of things have assumed their place as important; things that perhaps would have gone neglected, unnoticed, or without celebration. Because of my internal agony and my struggle for validation, every stitch of hope inside of me, when realized, must be greeted with applause, even if by the hands of one.

I continue daily to struggle to love others without cause, without expectation and without condition in spite of their actions. I work diligently to distance myself from the likeness of my father. There are moments during my life when all appears well and others when the battle seems lost. My mind reverts to the tiny room, and again and again I hear my mother and father's voices, reaching a fever pitch of anger and hurting. As the seasons come and go, I wrestle with angst as to what will be the final disposition of my life as it regards the impression of compassion that I have fought to offer others. I want the recollection of me to be one who had healed and led others to healing, and not the one who perpetuated distance and unfeeling.

I look at my daughters from afar as they play, enjoying small freedoms of which I knew not as a child. I speak a conscious word to myself to go forward and be involved in their lives; making every attempt at being a loving father; a foreign ideal to me. As depression grabs me about my ankles and pulls my face beneath the surface of life's waters, I literally struggle for breath on some days, needing desperately to hear one of my children say "I love you daddy." They bear a tremendous burden unknown to them. They are the very reason I continue to fight the demons of yesterday, the causes of my emotional relief, and the intermission betwixt my grief.

As I consider brokenness, I find it an amazing characterization for a man bred in violence and subsumed in a world of hyper-masculinity. It is an admission that the presentation of self is a dramatic production of an internal failure. In my humility, I know the true source from which my low self-portrayal has its roots. Yet, I embrace it, because my hunger to be successful, to matter, to change the lives of others, remains as insatiable and intense as the first pain I knew at the hands of my parents. It is a thorn I begrudgingly welcome; not thinking too much of myself, but celebrating each victory all the more because no one thought it possible.

These simple admissions of human frailty are neither enough, nor are they sufficient. They must be properly framed. They persist because in order to be a vessel for God's purposes. I understood long ago that the proficiencies and capabilities for which I am respected render me useless. I must decrease, that

He might increase in me. Only then have I made some assurance that my suffering has not been in vain. When I am fatigued with accusations, false witness and provocation, I am gently reminded that no indignity that I suffer could compare with the ultimate propitiation for my life eternal. For such a gift I willfully submit myself to remain tattered and still broken.

ADULT STAGE: The Metamorphosis

In the adult stage, it is said that the period for growth is over, but it is in fact the period that the world refers to as the butterfly stage. The butterfly flies from flower to flower in search of an optimal place to lay eggs. The life span of a butterfly spans but a few months, and yet we regard them as among the most beautiful of God's creatures because of their bright radiant hues, as they coast the breezes of summer. Many of us give chase out of curiosity, some capture, under the cloak of collecting, but it is truly misguided envy. We want to possess this beauty and somehow impute it into our own lives. It is the morphing of something superficially repulsive into an entity so overtly breath-taking and given a gift not even entrusted to man that ensnares me; flying.

In the chapters that follow, the principles are found that undergird the metamorphosis that I am experiencing. These six cherished concepts have taken me from contemplating and inviting death, to possessing a zest for this life; from being an integral part of the problem, to being sought out for solutions; from the doorstep of disaster to the mount of triumph, and in no way is my work done. My journey is not complete, unless those who have suffered the same indignities and self-destructive behaviors that I have can draw strength from this narrative offering. I will be chastised for such intimate disclosures, and rest assured that there is much more that cannot fit into the pages of this edict. Yet, I have been commissioned by an authority higher than any earthly decision-maker to give freely of my heart in this manner so that the lineage of butterflies might continue and the scenery of the earth might be continually populated with the beauty of unsuspecting origins.

CHAPTER 12: REDEMPTION

Sometimes I sit silently by an open window, breathing deeply, with a warmth inside that only men who have been behind bars can identify with. The sky is overcast and the sun has retreated. Thunder plays drums like the rhythm of the motherland, and lightening pierces the sky as rays of precise judgment. Finally, the tears of the heavens pound the streets, purging it of its iniquities for a time. The ground breathes a sigh of relief by way of steam, and the flowers do all that they can to withstand their sustenance. This is the first time in my life that I can truly appreciate the rain. It is a time of silence, a time of reflection, a time for God to cleanse His creation and His tiniest creatures. I find no need of a jacket, as I venture out and allow the rain to run rampantly down my face. I am in need of redemption. I have destroyed so much, hurt so many; been an enemy to many and a friend to few. It is for this reason that I hunger for redemption and thirst for righteousness. I know that my life is not my own any longer. I must sew a seed of hope and articulate the anguish of regret, so that the youth of tomorrow don't war against themselves in vain.

I guess that I spent so much precious time attempting to extinguish my being that now that I have tasted my purpose, I feel as though there is little time left to make amends. Today I speak to young gang members and work with ex-offenders in hopes of purging my own mind and realizing flight. The heart that once was an axis of evil all its' own, now aches for my brothers that refuse to heed my, nor Tookie Williams' words.

There were so many instances in which I made wasteful decisions and spent frivolously on the pleasures of a world that only loved me when I was its' pawn. Today, I long for a fraction of those funds to simply provide work for the men I work with. The roads we choose to travel many times lead to our demise. If we are blessed enough, we are granted time for suffering; for this is the incipience of the elusive concept of redemption.

The concept of redemption in the definitive sense quite simply means to restore or to return to a previous state of being. I have come into the full knowledge that to simply be restored is not sufficient, nor does it satiate the appetite of one whom has known the deprivation of self. I am constantly on a quest to become far more than I ever was before, as the being that I have been is one of which I am not proud, nor the mirror image of what I aspire to. Were it possible, perhaps I would dissociate myself from my former life, and walk steadfast into the destiny that I now embrace. Even now, as I am overwhelmed on most days with the regrets of my transgressions, I accept that they were a part of the journey towards fulfillment. Had I not sunk to the depths of negativity and absolute destitution, I could not now or ever appreciate the metamorphosis that has and is occurring.

One of the most difficult feats that one can face is the act of forgiveness. This concept is such a foreign ideal, because I know as you read this, you believe that I mean forgiving those who have hurt you. This is but partly true, as I am primarily discussing the notion of self-purging. Many of the scars that we bear as stigmata of having been harmed are intrinsic and are accompanied with one of the inquiries that began this book, "what did I do to deserve this?" Whether it was abuse of a sexual, emotional or physical nature, neglect or otherwise, it is very natural to begin with the assignment of blame. This is likely because, to do so is symptomatic of abuse and the fictitious rationalizations that remove guilt from perpetrators of this kind.

I take this opportunity to proclaim to you that nothing you did warranted your being harmed and it is not your fault. To the young girl who was molested or raped, it was not the way you dressed. To the young man that carries upon his heart a callous from the departure or absence of your father, you were not a "bad" child or any other indictment on your person that your cognition has tried to resolve for all of the years subsequent to your trauma. By coming to understand that basic and seemingly concealed truth, you begin the journey from victim to advocate. Wherever your pain lies, it can no longer control your life once you acknowledge it and expose it. We must endeavor to bare our scars, in so that someone in some corner of the earth is made free by our bravery.

Throughout the course of our lives, we encounter callous individuals that we believe purposely set out to hurt us and have no regard for our lives nor liberties. Newspaper headlines are bombarded with instances and accounts of unspeakable and heinous tragedies where lives are taken without warning or reason, small children are not spared the most savage of indignities and their innocence is taken and their lives muted. In the sanctity of our homes and romantic relationships we are deeply committed to the notion that there are social scripts that we are to follow, and even more, a particular way in which we ought to be treated. When these expectations are not met, or worse even, we are maltreated, we internalize feelings of not only bitterness towards the person that caused our heartache, but to a great extent ourselves.

Perhaps you would be more comfortable were I discussing how to forgive others, but there are a million other books that speak on such matters and this work and its parallel journey is about you. I am asking that you now resume "your life" as opposed to waiting for an apology or grand admission of guilt from someone who may never be capable of doing so. I have travelled the road of hope for acknowledgement, and I can tell you with all certainty that if it fails, it is more painful than the actual event(s). Have I forgiven? Indeed I have. I find a strange but real solace in having done so, and to an extent empowered. The point at which I feel the most free is when I humble myself in front of an audience and revisit my harm. At first it is a violent jostle of kindred aching that delays the collective breathing of all who suffer in silence, and all at once, it is replaced with a healing breeze.

We mistakenly assume that we can forget what has happened and notwithstanding we may for a time do exactly that. However, repressed memories are like both time bombs and hidden residue; it is but a matter of time before they explode or manifest themselves as a greater issue. I am in no way dismissive of your hurt, anger or resentment. I am in turn offering that, subconsciously, we most often turn our vengeance inward and rail against ourselves. Moreover, I am not advocating hyper-vigilance to repay the one who has wounded you so deeply; to do so would re-victimize you and make you as depraved and indifferent as the offender. Lastly, by all means, you must resist with all of your being, the statistical propensity to allow your trauma to become a cyclical phenomenon.

We tend to rationalize that repeated treatment of these sorts dictates that we are not worthy of love and caring. I can't tell you for how long I behaved in a manner that was nothing more than self-fulfilling prophecy. At the time when I was growing up, it was almost a statistical certainty that black males would die or go to prison by the age of 22. Needless to say, I realize that my disdain for life and others, coupled with a lifestyle of immediacy was because (1) I deeply feared those predictions regarding my demographic and more importantly, because of my traumatic rearing, (2) I felt as though my life had no worth. I blamed myself for a great number of things that I viewed through my youthful eyes.

I had come to possess a deep-seated hostility for myself, and involved myself in risk-taking behaviors in an effort to extinguish my life. As the loathing grew more intense through failure, so did the longing to die. It was at this point that I had garnered the courage to begin attempting suicide. After years of studies and introspection, I am able to critically analyze those thoughts and feelings therapeutically. I constantly adjudicated myself; and the same transgressions that others held against me, I too held against myself. Forgiveness of others was such a foreign ideal in my unrelenting heart that I couldn't forgive myself for my historical bad acts.

I constantly berated myself and refused to accept laudatory comments from others. I rationalized that there simply existed an ulterior motive, and the individual was attempting to get close to me and cause me some emotional harm. Even my perception of how I looked was unequivocally low. I found it unfathomable when I encountered narcissistic personalities. In my eyes, I was an unredeemable soul that was deserving of my mounting suffering.

The danger here is that, this self-dejection and hatred of self becomes cyclical until it not only affects one's self-portrait, but eventually manifests itself as problematic health. During those years of fast living in the streets, and witnessing unspeakable acts of violence and drug addiction that I contributed to, I developed stomach ulcers. The subculture in which I was involved, dictated that no one speak about their feelings; we weren't supposed to feel anything, as it made survival most difficult. Spontaneous incidences of violence and proving physicality even within our circle demonstrated that we couldn't truly trust one another. There in the midst, as are a great deal of our young men, I found myself in a dichotomy of responses: loyalty or betrayal. These were my choices, to go along without regard for consequence, or to risk the rejection of my peers whom I sorely needed for the development of an identity.

I think back on some of the vile things that we did, and until this day, I can provide no substantive explanation for my actions. As I began to move towards changing my life in the latter years, I realized that I had not forgiven myself for those horrors. I discovered that when I believed that I had achieved a nook of contentment, the past had an eerie way of intruding without notice, particularly during my sleep. I have had countless dreams of actual things that I have done, and perhaps even more about retaliations for the wrongs I have perpetrated. As I go out and speak to young men from time to time, I am sure to inform them that there is no end to what they do today. However, if change is to be authentic, then the act of penance must precede self-assessment.

Once I began to embrace the notion that I stood in no greater position than God with regards to forgiveness, I was able to move forward in a more positive direction. In simplistic terms, who was I to hold myself morally hostage when my faith dictated to me that all I need do was simply ask with contrite heart to be forgiven, and it would then be so. The next step in my personal voyage would dictate that I find something about myself that was a redeemable quality. This was in effect, a more involved endeavor than articulated. I had exhausted myself in such a constant state of negativity, that I had never truly evaluated my talents, skills, competencies or capacities.

I began to search inwardly, as opposed to seeking of others, for the qualities that made me revered and liked in the streets, and concluded that character assets are tools that are forged into either weaponry or used as instruments towards honorable ends. Once I took an honest inventory of both my character and the repertoire of employable skills that I possessed, I knew almost at once that things were destined to turn around somehow. I would be at the least dishonest if I said that I forged ahead from this point without impediment.

I recall tracking the final months of the life of Stanley "Tookie" Williams, and reading some of his literature, in which he beckoned young people either already involved in gang activity or contemplating it, to stop the killing and senseless violence, and instead pursue worthwhile exploits. He called his latter years his personal pursuit of "redemption." A plethora of his words struck a chord deep within me. While I had long since distanced myself from active gang involvement and overt acts of violence, I thought a great deal about redemption.

Redemption to me was a peculiar oddity. It dictated that I challenge myself on such tenets as, "what was my debt to society; what was my charge to keep?" "Tookie" had by his own efforts at redemption placed me in an uncomfortable conundrum. I had to fully contemplate the parallels between who I was born to be, and who I was resolved to be. I found them to be one in the same. We are conditioned to measure opportunity and the lack thereof by the ideals of society. Hence we acquiesce into fixed realities and labor there, according to what is commonplace, never really exploring the possibilities.

As you strive to free yourself, peer deep beyond the surface into your humanity and determine whether or not you are guided by your confines, or by potentialities. As a young boy, I had planned my life far in advance and had situated myself as a civil rights attorney in my dreams. I was determined to fight against injustice and racism, just as my childhood idols, born of the aforementioned period. I took the necessary steps to become a superior orator and spent much of my time, reading and writing unlike my peers that were allowed to play outside unbridled. If allowed to gaze into the future, no one could convince me of what my eyes would behold.

Those years in and out of penal institutions and fighting for my actual survival led me to believe that there was no way possible for me to realize those ambitions of old. There was no way that I would ever become a lawyer now. I thought of my existence as finding work that I was resolved to do. I worked in fast food for the most part, and saw no escape from the grind of financial mediocrity and task-oriented redundancy. All of my preparations and good grades had been in vain. I used to refer to myself as "an ex-could've been great."

I likened myself to basketball star, Len Bias; a bright star that was preparing to set the world aglow and had been vanquished while standing on the brink of greatness and never crossed over into that place called fruition. It was not until I read the story of Joseph in the Bible that my life began to make sense. We are not all accomplished by conventional methods.

Pain and heartache along with the unforeseen and unintended are still purposed. In fact, by definition, the concept of redemption predicates that something unfortunate must happen to begin the long road back to what is meant to be. I often think of how many dreams go unrealized because we are bound by confines. I had a friend comment to me on one occasion that we can't simply think outside of the box, "we have to think as though there is no box", he added. Culture is that variable that envelops us during our youth. It is often guised as reality by peers and even adults who have failed to achieve the same ends. In their defense, I think that they rationalize that they have spared us the pain of their disappointment. It is entirely up to you as to how you deal with naysayers. I choose to learn from their mistakes. The first of which was perhaps to think of their dream as some long shot or impossibility that existed in a world of fantasy and just maybe under a special set of circumstances.

As I have matured spiritually and socially, I now know that there is nothing that I cannot achieve. I have been gifted in so many ways, that to even contemplate failure would undermine my very existence. I made the decision to place myself in positions where the outcome would not avail much. The focus and determination that I have now is born of both urgency and expectancy; an urgency and expectancy to succeed. In addition, while I struggle with it sometimes, I have to some extent learned to love myself and counted myself worthy of good things. I have forgiven myself, knowing full well that I have been redeemed of my transgressions and trespasses.

I have also forgiven "Him". This allegory would be meaningless and hypocritical had I not yet arrived at a point where I could say that I do not blame my father for the trespasses of my youth, or my adulthood for that matter. I no longer blame my mother for her inability to remove us all from the terrors of yesteryear. I love them both for having given life to me, and I can honestly say that I have forgiven them. I came to recognize that the unwillingness or inability to forgive disqualified me for the same measure of grace, and even more, relegated me to still being a victim. I could no longer bear that weight upon my shoulders; it was emotionally and cognitively draining.

Sometimes I become weary and even take things for granted as I ride this carousel that is life. I bare constant reminders on my wrists that this life is not over until God says that it is, and until I have done all that He has called me to do for the men that I was sent to serve. You cannot kill that which is destined to live. I have written many times that "one cannot be so fleet of foot, as to outrun destiny." It is with the aforementioned lessons that I have appraised my worth, and found myself a candidate for this thing called redemption.

CHAPTER 13: VISIONARY

Subsequent to the realization that I was deserving of the fullness of life and joy, (note that I did not say happiness) I had to make some sense of an uncertain future. The opposite of order is chaos. I had lived in chaos for over two decades, and found only crevices of happiness. Happiness is fleeting and instantaneous, and even awaiting another emotion to fill its place. Joy is something eternal that cannot be penetrated by situations, people or contexts. In order to attain the promise for my life, I knew that I could not reassume the path, or the nefarious activities that had taken away my physical freedom, and tarnished my dreams. I also knew that I had to distance myself from both the influences and the people that had ultimately helped lead to my disposition.

As I spent time awaiting my release from the military brig, I initially languished within my surroundings and became depressed and was constantly visited by suicidal ideation. I could not fathom how I had come to be in the situation in which I found myself. While life had been thus far a bitter experience, I never imagined that I would lose years of my life to the criminal justice system. I then made the conscious decision not to. Here is where the incipience of renaissance began for me.

As I poured myself into titles, at the urging of "Godfather", what I simultaneously learned was that while my body was a trapped vessel bound by iron and steel, my mind was always free to leave. I became so many literary characters, traveled the world and commanded the English language. My imagination was like that of a child playing alone outside. Imagery and fantasy were my playgrounds, never to be trespassed upon by the reality of prison yards and clanging cell doors. As I made my escape, sunrises had never been so radiant, rain never so refreshing, and clouds never so mystifying.

I truly gained an appreciation for the world and its inhabitants, both of person and of nature. Books helped me greatly prepare myself for a world outside of this place. During my incarceration there were no programs in which I was eligible to participate, nor did anyone apprise me of the concept of re-entry services. Some begin with the premise that "failure is not an option" upon release; I laud that. However, I assumed the cognitive posture that succeeding was not only paramount, but must be done so overwhelmingly.

The latter portion of my time in the brig was spent crafting letters and requesting transcripts to attend college. I had always been a good student; school just seemed to come easy for me. Someone once imparted to me that your opinion on matters carries with it little to no credibility until you are measured by the standards of the system in which you wish to operate. That understanding guided my decision to abide by the rules and pursue higher education. I was later accepted to college and went on to finish my degree in a period of two and one half years. This would equate to the exact quantity of time that I spent in prisons and jails. I went to school year round and full-time with my toddler son living in the dorm and eating in the cafeteria unbeknownst to school officials.

I had planned to pursue employment opportunities subsequent to graduation and see where that led. I successfully landed a job through a friend that knew of my past and gave me an opportunity. The same pattern would follow for about two years. One day while at work, a co-worker mentioned a Master's Program to me at another local university. I looked into it and was quickly accepted and did exceptionally well, finishing that degree in two years while working and rearing my son. During that time, I was hit with a barrage of dreams about future businesses and opportunities, how they should be run and in which industries they should be. I was so compelled by the meticulous nature of the dreams that I stayed up for close to two days straight pecking out the details on a word processor.

I had not yet attained the maturity or wisdom to understand what was transpiring within my dreams. Now, more than a decade later, I surmise that those dreams were premonitions into my future. It is imperative that I note that all of the visions that I had were not specifically for me to perform, but they were indeed all things that have become tangible realities in one form or another. So often, people perform an act called proof-texting. What this means is that they utilize the Bible or the Koran as the ultimate authority to substantiate what they believe to be true, or to condone behavior that is ultimately flawed. The reason that I mention this is that, for many years people made every effort to speak things into my life and to offer me their analysis of my dreams and visions, and even ones that they had about me.

Over and over again, people would interpret that my dreams were born of a scripture found in the book of Habakkuk: 2, which cites that we should write the vision and make it plain. I accepted most of what I heard, over and over again believing that I would personally own and operate everything that I saw in those visions years ago. My belief was based on the fact that I had never taken the time to read the passage for myself. The entirety of the scripture goes on to offer, "That he may run who reads it. For the vision is for an appointed time; but at the end it will speak, and it will not lie. Though it tarries, wait for it." As I focused my attention on the latter portion of the scripture, I was granted interpretation, and I could effectively plan for the next phase of my future.

I study the successful individuals of this day, and tend towards concentrating on how they handle adversity. I am sure that they don't plan for any of their business endeavors to fail, but alternatively, I am all but certain that there are contingencies throughout the plan that still lead to the ultimate goal. I plan to succeed, that I might well know how to handle it gracefully and humbly. I also plan to encounter stumbling blocks and inhibitions along the way, so that I do not waste a great deal of time tied up in the disappointment of having to regroup.

I have also come to understand through a more thorough understanding of the scripture, that simply because I am the visionary, I am not necessarily the individual chosen to accomplish the work. Previously I would become frustrated because some grand epiphany had not yet come into being, and that perhaps I had misunderstood or misinterpreted the vision. Instead, I have learned that God has equipped others with talents and skill sets that are not visionaries, but instead are actuators and follow instructions to the letter. This required that I relinquish my perceived ownership of divine works, and be graciously accepting of the role entrusted to me by God with all humility.

In the fall of 2007, I had the humbling experience of speaking to graduates of a re-entry program at Forsyth Detention Center in Winston Salem, North Carolina. While they abashed me with conciliatory comments, the one thing that I recall being a recurring theme that day was making use of the time. There is no commodity so rich as time. I had learned this lesson two times over with the loss of my grandparents. Time cannot be purchased, nor can it be bartered for. Once time has expired, it cannot be recaptured. It is the one thing that the human spirit rails against with all of its being. We are unable to manipulate it, and it is the one standard in our lives that refuses to bow to whim. Perhaps, this is why doing time, or being incarcerated is so painful to the soul of a man. Needless to say, I am saddened most often by the notion that I did not achieve more during my time incarcerated. I beseech you that you are not held in abeyance, but that your mind quickly reconciles that while the body must, the mind can never rest.

As a reader of this book, it would serve you well, to write out at length, goals; how you plan to achieve them, and timetables for your success. I reiterate that contingency planning should always be accounted for, so that the emotions associated with being told "no" or "not right now" doesn't cripple the vision. I am uncertain of where I might find myself now were it not for adversity. I might not be as meticulous and careful in my work had I not been rebuffed. I always tell my students to give their very best effort each and every time that their name is attached to something, offering that they pursue absolute perfection. If the aim is perfection, then failure parallels some semblance of excellence.

While I cannot speak to the challenges that befall other demographics upon their release from places of incarceration, young black men return to a likely eventuality of cyclical recidivism. Philosophically, it is the establishment of a stance that in the face of failure, unemployment, lack of support and potentially even hunger, the former lifestyle is not even considered in the repertoire of coping mechanisms.

There have been so many days that I wanted to lie down in the middle of this journey and give up my being. It was however the understanding that the things to which I aspired needed to be conquered not merely for myself, but for men that had not yet been released, to remove all excuses for failure. In my mind's eye, failure is defined as having never tried. Many young men return from penal facilities and die innumerable deaths having shared their dreams with another and told they were preposterous given their circumstance. Thus my measure of success was pre-mandated for those yet to be ensnared by the trappings of this world.

I transcend my memories and attempt to empathize with the disposition of my captive ancestors who first dreamt of freedom. I can hear their voices in a heated exchange, whereby one has decided that a life of vile treatment and familial degradation is no life at all, while yet another slave speaks with fierce trepidation warning him that his lot will be much worse if his plan is discovered, or worse if he is caught. The great-grandsons born of his willingness to simply try are faced with a distant parallel and disjointed from the hope of his spirit. It is so with the first to take flight, the first to challenge a tradition, the first to barter his life for a cause greater than himself; there will always be detractors that err on the side of misnomer and innuendo. I believe for this purpose, was I born. I needed sorely to try and to fail and to try again.

I will never forget the story of how one of the most accomplished men in our program sought work while living in the half-way house upon his release. He shared that he had gone to apply for a job, and the secretary maltreated him, essentially as if he were a "nobody". He was still kind, knowing full well that he was not in a position to be sidetracked by pettiness. He sat in that office for four hours waiting for the manager to come and speak with him. He was then apprised that the manager had left for lunch and that he would need to return in an hour or two. He returned promptly after the manager's lunch hour, only to be told "no" in a rather harsh tone. My heart ached for him, and secretly tears began to well in my eyes, because I knew firsthand how cruel and unforgiving society can be at times. I was then astonished to hear him say that he walked almost 50 minutes to another job to apply. His words to me that day were, "Doc, out of 100 jobs that tell me no, one person is going to say yes, and I promise I am going to work harder than any three men they have for less pay."

He already had a contingency plan. In fact he had 99 of them, according to his statistics. What if he had thrown his hands up, and returned to his former lifestyle after the tenth "no", or even the twentieth; not knowing if the eleventh or the twenty-first was his "yes"? Today, he is an entrepreneur, holds three part-time jobs and a full-time job, has gained custody of his children, and owns a new home and four vehicles. He accomplished all of these goals within one and a half years of being released into the care of a half-way house.

I stand in awe of his accomplishments, but more importantly, I take note of his formula for success. He simply says, "I envisioned all of this in prison, and I refuse to be denied a good life." Deferment is surely not denial, and abandoning your dream should never be an option. If you have ever been fortunate enough to dream, then it is always within your grasp. Visions are supernatural gifts, given to those equipped with the knowledge of their direction, that require little more than whole-hearted belief and sustained effort in order that they might come into fruition.

CHAPTER 14: MOTIVATION

A peculiar challenge to me has become the discerning of modalities to employ in order to motivate differing personality types. For some, motivation is a derivative of an outside source, while some garner motivation from within. Personally, I achieve motivation through the disbelief in my lofty expectations from others. I am driven to succeed by individuals that have all but discarded me. The trials of this walk have nearly torn my soul from my being. I once thought the pain of disappointment and failures were incomparable, until I came face to face with the pain associated with success. The man that is revered is oft hated, not because he thinks too much of himself, but he was once small in the minds of others, and now they are unable to compel him back to such insignificance; some refer to them as "haters" or "naysayers", but I call them "grounding forces". These are entities in our lives that masquerade as friends, promising relationships or concerned relatives. In actuality they are the very things or persons that deter us from flight.

It is inconceivable of how many times that it has been commented to me that "You changed", "You ain't real no more" or "You're doing too much." I have poured my heart and mind into fighting the good fight for others, in trying to prove what can be done if a man is afforded half a chance. In staying tangible to those returning home from prison, the accomplishments that I consider to be minimal achievements have polluted the pledges of loyalty, have undermined the greater vision, and have driven men apart that were intended to set ablaze the sky and restructure urban landscapes. I have grown weary of pouring my spirit into men who want little more than mediocrity. I have instead befriended but a handful, and ultimately hold close my own friendship. I still talk to myself. I urge myself to hark unto the winds of yesterday that carry upon its shoulders my childhood aspirations of greatness.

It is so difficult to bear in one ear the seeds of discontent and on the lobe of the other the kiss of Judas, especially when it falls from the lips of a loved one. I have been paralyzed at times with incredulity pertaining to the purposeful destruction of the hope one's sleeve is adorned with. I count myself no less of a man to say that my heart has actually been broken by the indescribable ought that men garner in their hearts "while the other fellow stars". It is not the expectation that lacks; it is equivocal effort. I count myself no greater than any other, until there is discussion regarding multi-tasking and effort. I plainly compete with myself. I know of no other being that has at heart my own self-interest to the extent that I do.

I am eager to outdo my former effort at every turn, while making sure that every effort is the very best that I have to offer. The perfect enigma that I create is an inability to be satisfied and a desire to keep trying. As long as there is breath in my body, I cannot give up trying to be better, do better and make others better. My day begins as a surprise, because I know not how my days are numbered. I intently thank God before my feet touch the floor, and I pursue victory in all things at all costs. Another oddity that has little to do with my present character, but who I have been purposed to be, is that somewhere down the road, along life's journey, I have blessed those that sought to use or devour me. The very individuals that wish me ill and long for my downfall have found that I have departed their company and left them with some favor or minute piece of money. All the while they believe that they have gotten over, that they have performed some grand coup, never quite understanding the friend they've lost, or the measure of heart given unto me.

To say that these things do not take a toll on my humanity and disgust me to the point of feeling foolish, would be prevarications and outright lies; after all I am but a man. Ultimately, I console myself with the notion that greater things lie ahead, of which this person could not be a part, and recollect them in recluse. The dimensions of grace that come subsequent to these endeavors are okay, but I am most proud of having refused to react to these transgressions as my former self.

Hence, they motivate me to keep pressing forward. I am unsure of where I am destined to conclude this journey, or what the world will have to comment on as to what I have contributed it, but the one thing of which I am certain, people's contexts and conceptualizations of inducements towards the affirmative are forever changed having made my acquaintance. He, whom best motivates me, resides in the mirror.

CHAPTER 15: ATTITUDE

"The longer I live, the more I realize the impact of attitude on life. It is more important than the past, than education, than money, than circumstances, than failures, than successes, than what other people think or say or do. It is more important than appearance, giftedness or skill. It will make or break a company ... a church ... a home. The remarkable thing is we have a choice every day regarding the attitude we will embrace for that day. We cannot change our past ... we cannot change the fact that people will act in a certain way. We cannot change the inevitable. The only thing we can do is play on the one string we have, and that is our attitude... I am convinced that life is 10% what happens to me and 90% how I react to it. And so it is with you ... we are in charge of our attitude."
- Chuck Swindoll

One of the easiest things to do in life is to allow failures and negativity to beset us as we march towards any goal that we sorely covet. It is our nature to voice frustration when things go awry, and further attempt to frame the underlying rationale as to why we have been rejected or fallen short once again. All about us there are some people who endeavor to smile and perceive their circumstance as "half full". As I have broadened my studies to encompass a global lens, the condition of our world beckons us to contrast our realities. It is when I consider that my shoes are merely worn, when others are without limbs; or when I recall being hungry while food awaits me unprepared, while others die of starvation; or when I pitied myself for having been homeless and in the country of Darfur one half of a million people are walking across a desert with all that they own upon their frail backs, simply to prevent the rape of their children and the extermination of their race, I can find no good reason for which to complain.

Mental tenacity abounds out of necessity. A man is his strongest when he focuses not on his circumstance, but on the solution. One of the greatest achievements in my life, of which I do not boast, is merely remaining strong enough to stay my hand from taking my life. When you have encountered your darkest hour and summarily characterize it as a learning experience, it is at that very instance that you have grown as a person and seized control of your fate. Many would have you to feel as though you were less than, or in some manner inferior because of an experience that you have endured. Nothing could be more distant from the truth. When others portray occurrences as negative, do you have the wherewithal to humbly seek the lesson? As opposed to asking "Why is this happening to me" or "For how long must I endure this particular suffering?" I have instead grown to ask, "What have I been purposed to learn from this?"

I no longer regard incidents as negative, for to do so would lend myself to an emotion that, when all has been weighed, has no bearing on the outcome. There was a time in my life when I believed that life and all of its contortions were happening to me. In sharp contrast now, I look upon tribulations as proving grounds and modalities through which I might expand my repertoire of coping alternatives. My mind has become more sharpened and focused because of trials. I refuse to falter, or to ever again attempt to assassinate the grand purpose for which I was birthed.

As hurdles arise in my daily life, I simply pause and begin taking deep breaths; an art I had never considered during my teenage years. It is a process that allows me to take inventory of not only the players in the moment, but of myself. I now understand that being reactionary increases the probability to find myself in less than optimal positions. I would be lying if I said that life's hurdles have not brought me to my knees at times. However, such circumstances, in which I cannot maneuver, increase the virtue of patience, which I never before possessed. When the self is exposed, the lesson becomes clear. I've found that there is typically some behavior or undesirable trait that is being disbanded through the experience.

Ultimately the overarching, yet simplistic, goal in life is to be looked upon as a good and decent person. Possessing a positive attitude and speaking that positivity into the lives of others is what overwhelmingly determines this measure. When people spoke of Buddy, they often cited that "He never met a stranger" and the lasting impression of him in my mind is always with a smile fixated upon his countenance. What would I have become had he not sown seeds of love and positivity into my existence? My smile is a testament to his life here on earth. Even when I don't feel like it sometimes I force a smile in the direction of someone who looks like I feel, and we are both the better for it.

I tend to be amused by individuals who hold fast to superstition, believing that one socially constructed faux pas or culturally contrived misstep might lend them to being cursed or change their luck for the worst. I've never believed in such things, but to those who do, I present that the same manner in which you are able to speak and think negativity and witness them birthed into fruition, should be consistent with the antithesis. Surely, the same mind and mouth can contemplate goodness and utter words of resolve that should too evolve into good fortune. When I can see no good thing on the horizon, I simply hunker down and usher into my mind the images of those who by no fault of their own suffer plights far greater. I then reckon that even if things fail to get better by my standards, I have already received two lifetimes of mercies.

Lastly, one of the most interesting things about our trials is that often we have our own issues resolved while altruistically performing in the service of others. It is the evolving concern of individualism that has polluted our sense of community, placing us at odds with one another, assuring that conflict abounds. It is vitally important that you discover and consistently maintain entities in your life that serve as light to your soul that can rinse from you the morass of pains and disappointments with simple gestures of kindness and reassurance. Moreover, you must strive with all strivings to give that gift in return. Above all things though, we must change our *attitudes*.

CHAPTER 16: SUCCESS

Perhaps the most enticing question that might be asked at the outset of this section is, "How is success defined?" It is purely subjective and rests with the drives that find haven within the hearts of men. Most assuredly, "to each according to his ability" may readily come to mind, but I find this to be a practical falsehood. It is not the case that the most gifted or talented among us attains the greatest measure of success. It is indeed he whom develops a plan and executes it with precision, taking stock of the things that have served as impediments along his way. In simpler terms, as men such as myself begin the long road back to redemption, it is important to stop along the way, and make note of the methods that we employ that actually yield fruit.

According to Jack Mack Carter, "When you have much success, two things happen; the first is that we begin to take success for granted. The second is that we forget how we got here—namely, by exceptionally hard work and in spite of intense competition." One major impediment that is born of the lifestyle chronicled within this book is the notion that the one who is successful can quantify his success by tangible acquisitions. One of the passages that readily barrels through my mind is, "What does it profit a man to gain the world yet lose his own soul?"

As we sat on stoops and porches in the housing projects watching sports cars zoom by, we played a game called "Mine-A-Time", which entailed waiting for traffic to approach and being the first to claim a "hot" car. I think more so than anything we relished and coveted the inference made about the people that were passengers in those cars. "Man, they must have a great life", I thought. We struggled just to put enough change together to buy popsicles from the ice cream man. We pledged as kids that one day we would finally live the "good life". Many of my childhood friends died utilizing unconventional and illegal methods pursuing the "good life".

As I began to amass things, I began to understand the words of a fallen hip hop star by the name of Biggie Smalls warning, "More money more problems". Those words fell on deaf ears of a generation trying relentlessly to wear his shoes. The mentality of my peers had always been that the problems would be well worth it, as long as we no longer had to live on our knees. For most of us, being ethical or principled never entered the equation; success for us meant having "stuff" at all costs. I've come to learn that the cost of mammon is inordinately higher than any of us can fathom, and is not an adequate measure of true success.

Success in my opinion is embedded in the process, not the manifestation. Many people count themselves as having failed because in contrast they did not achieve the same measure of success that another did. Success is purely subjective. As I think back on the simplistic lifestyles of both of my grandmothers, I can recall both of them being immensely focused on the life beyond this one. To them, treating people with common courtesy and dignity warranted them being treated the way that the wealthy long for. When money was in short supply or when my grandmother was unsure of where her very next meal would come from, she would sit on the same couch that followed her from the projects into her new home and simply hum and smile. It was I that began doing illegal things to provide for her when she knew that God already had. The model of success that I borrowed from both of their lives was of being a person of integrity, kind-hearted and the voice of reason and chastity among my family. If I can but find the wherewithal to climb such mountains with a smile of serenity genuinely fixated upon my face, then I have been successful.

CHAPTER 17: LOVE

"And now abideth faith, hope, love, these three; but the greatest of these is love."
−1 Corinthians 13:13.

It is oft said that one can never truly love another unless first he loves himself. I have always and perhaps will always adamantly disagree. Throughout this work, I have chronicled my disdain for myself, as well as the apathetic and barbaric manner in which I once lived. It was in fact the "streets" unwritten rules of behavior that taught me to respect the innocence of small children and reverence the wisdom of the elders. Those were two tenets that I never questioned. In moments of cognitive sobriety, when my heart was polluted with self-hatred and vengeful rage, I watched children play, wishing for a semblance of their innocence, and at the other end of the continuum, I watched as the elderly struggled to live quiet and peaceable lives.

Perhaps one day I might get that old, I thought. As suddenly as the dream entered my head, it vanished. I was betwixt two realities of which I was certain neither could be achieved.

Until the birth of my children, I realize in retrospect that I've never really loved myself. I grew to hate and be hated. It was in part, my defense mechanism. I was in dire pain and every action and reaction in which I have been engaged was an articulation of hurting. In my recent years, as a man of faith, I have been forced to redefine not only myself, but look candidly at my intrinsic disdain. I have no blame to dole out; not to "Him" or "Ma" or any circumstance that has visited my life. Again I say they have been carefully orchestrated to bring me to this point of having no fear in baring my soul in these pages. The journey has been indescribably painful and the dissipating of self-loathing is a rigorous surgical procedure.

As stray bullets threatened the innocence and solitude I sorely coveted, I realized that I and those like me are enemies unto ourselves. We were the real reason that neither could be achieved. We were boys that used childish methods to attain manhood and the capacity to bring cessation to our own lives is what we so desperately and subconsciously were barreling towards. As mothers reached for and prayed for me, and toddlers looked at me in a peculiar manner, I became more aware of their existence on our faux-battlefield. I say this to say that I first loved the young and the defenseless before I ever thought myself worthy of affection. It was not such a leap given that our code called for respect and reprieve for their existences.

When I finally stopped running from the beast within and sat in my cell, I could then vividly recall that thing for which I longed most urgently. One card, a partial letter or a phone call could set the world right again amidst my animalistic surroundings. These were the moments of tenderness that were true and guarded.

For some it is but temporary, but my change had begun and would be a definitive and marked process, where I would be forced to engage myself in dialogue between the foolish disappointment my life was now, and as the child I was, seemingly a lifetime ago. The child began to talk about dreams that I had and times when I was happy. No longer would I simply draw from the bitter recollections of those sleepless nights.

The child asked me why had I destroyed his future and why had I placed him at such great risk for even more harm. "Don't you love me?" he beckoned in my sleep. "Why did you bring me here?" he chided. I had forgotten what was good and innocent about myself. I was wallowing in the frigid turmoil of yesterday to the extent that I was blindly moving into the future looking backwards. I hated my upbringing so intensely that I cast out the teachings, the vision and the purpose for my life along with the repressed memories. It was my care and concern for the suffering of others that now purposed me and drove me. I wanted to champion equality, justice and life for my people, just as my childhood heroes had done.

It became more clairvoyant as I read and studied the lives of men like Malcolm, Gandhi, Garvey, DuBois, King and Mandela, that they were lovers of people and suffered from acute selflessness. Their lives were labors of love. Dr. King's words pang in my soul. When I have closed my eyes for the final time, I wish for someone to say, on that day, that Dr. Lewis "tried to love somebody." I went on to assure the young boy that if given half the chance, we too would love people into better conditions. We would fight with a vigor unmatched and never before seen. We would resist oppression with the remnant of the blood of slaves coursing hotly through our veins; walking boldly, professing in the affirmative that one man can make a difference, and willing to do so at all costs. Finally, as he departed my subconscious for the last time, the boy asked me plainly if I was certain and how I would respond to the question in the days and years to come about the concept of love. I responded in short and then with the words of Christ.

My life is not my own; I know nothing of the time and season given for it to end. I will not so callously disregard it, nor will I cling to it. I will instead return to my first works, presenting myself a living sacrifice for my neighbors, those whom I have been commanded to love as I love myself, for "greater love hath no man than this that a man lay down his life for his friends."

– John 15:13

CHAPTER 18: A MESSAGE OF HOPE

It is within your grasp to change the world, not simply your situation. If your mind can conceive of a thing, you have already begun the obligatory steps to transforming both your disposition and that of others. Bear in mind always that the final chapter of your life has not been written or for that matter determined. One instance cannot plot an entire life course. If you receive nothing else from the appraisal of this narrative, it should be that hope should forever abide in the soul of man, because all things are possible; even the impossible. I am running headlong into my destiny, with bated breath, gracefully accommodating for turbulence, having been purged by newly found self-efficacy; I am prepared to take flight and complete my metamorphosis.

Your existence resides not in the shadows of victimization, but in the brilliant luminescence of enlightened transparency. It is your responsibility to reach for new plateaus, soar towards new apexes and resist complacency at all costs. Whatever your plight has been, it does not belong to you singularly. Alternatively, you have been charged with leading a resurrection of others who have died unnecessary deaths of personhood. You must never rest until you have emerged victorious over temporary restraints, places of darkness, and/or uncertainty.

As long as there is breath in your body, there is hope; hope that things will not merely turn around but that you will transcend your wildest imaginations. Everyone dreams of being phenomenal in their own right. Along the way we are dissuaded by entrusting those fragile matters to individuals who never attempted flight. We allow them to vanquish the flame within us. We relent to their characterization of our nothingness, and we fail to evolve. When we are given a final resting place, someone speaks of our life as unrealized potential; never having permeated our place in the stratosphere. You must not fall prey to the threshold of people who adhere to the regiment that produces low expectations.

With every fiber of my being, I wish for you the most expeditious pathways to discovering your purpose and leaving a legacy of human worth. There is a shortage of genuinely good people on earth. I have penned this allegory for the bleakest soul on the planet, for the young mind contemplating suicide, the young man or woman crucifying their sleep with painful childhood memories, for the indigent resident of the coldest park bench, for the battered wife, those afraid of the darkness, the lonely, the child whose allegiance belongs to a family of colored bandanas, those with low self-esteem, the forgotten, the imprisoned, the recently released, for innocence lost, the unloved, those on the edge of perishing, for Buddy and Mama, for you and for me. If no other soul will relinquish to you the words withheld from me most of my life, then know that I will now without pause. I love you. You are a person of great worth. Your life truly matters. This is the message of hope that I beseech you to impart throughout the four corners of the world.

Your value cannot be overstated, nor can your existence be encapsulated in mere words. Conversely my friend, your deeds must preach when you can no longer speak for yourself. If you believe that this anecdote has been one of moral exhortation, then you have sorely missed the point. This volume has been a call to realize an internal utopia and share it with others. It has been a battle cry to rouse the champion that you are. Awaken to yourself and entreat yourself to the best that life has to offer. Seize from the pits of your soul a passion for life that is unparalleled.

There are some who believed that with every achievement since I emerged from confinement that I had reached the pinnacle of success. How pitifully wrong they were. I will forever continue to raise my own level of expectation, feeling and loving more deeply and truly. There are so many things that I long to achieve, to experience, to be, to render unto others. Why must there be ceiling on such things? We are but human; thus the path that shall ultimately lead us to prominence may not be the one popularly chosen, or the path of least resistance. As for my own, it is has been an insidious byway, but always towards the aim of flight. This is my story. I am desperately attempting to become the person that God sees me as. I am becoming a butterfly.

This Book Belongs
to Timothy Graham

Made in the USA
Lexington, KY
22 November 2012